Art in a Mirror

The Counterproofs of Mary Cassatt

Art in a

The Counterproofs of

Mirror

Mary Cassatt

FOREWORD BY

Warren Adelson

PREFACE BY

Marc Rosen and Susan Pinsky

ESSAYS BY

Jay E. Cantor

Pamela A. Ivinski

ADELSON GALLERIES   NEW YORK

In Memoriam:
Rita Rich Fraad (1915–2004)
who loved American art
and her fellow collectors and enthusiasts

Presented by

Marc Rosen Fine Art, Ltd.

220 EAST 73RD STREET
NEW YORK, NY 10021
TELEPHONE 212 535-5283
WWW.MARCROSENFINEART.COM

This book was published on the occasion of the exhibition

Art in a Mirror:
The Counterproofs of
Mary Cassatt

November 1, 2004, to January 14, 2005

Adelson Galleries

THE MARK HOTEL
25 EAST 77TH STREET
NEW YORK, NY 10021
TELEPHONE 212 439-6800
WWW.ADELSONGALLERIES.COM

ISBN 0-9741621-1-6

Library of Congress Control Number: 2004114526

Printed in the United States of America
10 9 8 7 6 5 4 3 2 1

Front cover:
Nude Dark-Eyed Little Girl with Mother
in Patterned Wrapper [detail of cat. 31, p. 97]

Contents

Foreword

After years of training in Europe as an academic painter, Mary Cassatt (1844–1926), a Pennsylvanian transplanted to Paris after the Civil War, became a colleague of Edgar Degas and discovered her path in modern art. It was in the atmosphere of Claude Monet's Impressionist revolution of the 1870s that she matured as an independent artist and worked in concert with the creators of "the new painting." She hung twelve works in the fourth Impressionist exhibition in 1879 and continued to exhibit with the radical group in the next decade. In 1880 she joined her friend and mentor Degas in a project to make original prints, and it was in this medium that she was to excel as the most daring and experimental of all her colleagues. In the little-used mediums of etching, soft ground, drypoint, and aquatint, Cassatt pulled black-and-white prints, first from Degas's press and then from one she acquired to use in her own studio. She began to achieve tonal harmonies and tactile linear effects in subjects taken from modern life.

A decade later, Cassatt was thrilled by the great exhibition of Japanese prints at the École des Beaux-Arts, a massive event with thousands of objects that was the talk of the art world on both sides of the Atlantic. Inspired by the brilliant color woodcuts of Hokusai, Utamaro, and other recorders of Japanese life, Cassatt produced ten aquatints with subjects derived from her own experience and observations, applying the color to the copper plates for each print herself and creating a luminous and haunting series that remains a landmark in the medium. These works became the highlight of her first one-person show at Galeries Durand-Ruel in 1891 and received critical and public acclaim. (Cassatt was Durand-Ruel's only American artist.)

By the turn of the century, Cassatt had established herself as a pivotal figure within the canon of modernism. She grew disenchanted with Durand-Ruel during this time, and began to work with the younger and more daring Ambroise Vollard, whose gallery in Montmartre had become the epicenter of cutting-edge art. Vollard loved the graphic arts and single-handedly created the marketplace for works on paper by painters, urging his artists—Pierre Bonnard, Paul Cézanne, Marc Chagall, Paul Gauguin, and Édouard Vuillard, as well as Pablo Picasso and Henri Matisse—to work in multiple images. Vollard understood Cassatt's restless experimentation and the summary nature of her work, and he enthusiastically purchased paintings and pastels that were thought to be too "unfinished" by the more conservative Durand-Ruel. It was in this context that the counterproofs in this exhibition were produced.

The unfolding of these events is brilliantly brought to life by Jay E. Cantor and Pamela A. Ivinski in the two essays contained in this publication. Marc Rosen and Susan Pinsky, the exhibition's producers, knew where these works had been kept. Through their efforts the trove has now been brought to light. We are grateful to them for their special insights and to the other people who have helped in the production of this unique event. William H. Gerdts contributed his wise counsel as a member of the Mary Cassatt Catalogue Raisonné Committee. Andrea Maltese has organized the production of the exhibition and this publication. Hubbard Toombs registered the collection, and my colleagues at Adelson Galleries have been attentive to every detail. They have my thanks.

WARREN ADELSON

Preface

Four years ago, we were excited by the opportunity to present, at Adelson Galleries, an extraordinary cache of prints and drawings from the studio of Mary Cassatt. Those recently discovered works greatly expanded our knowledge of the artist's activities in printmaking and provided a unique view into her artistic methods. We were made aware then of a small group of pastel counterproofs by Mary Cassatt, works whose production had been encouraged by Ambroise Vollard. We had only a brief glimpse at the time, but when these became available, we realized that here, too, was a rich repository of undisturbed pictures, a veritable time capsule from an earlier epoch. While going through the collection, set aside by Vollard so long ago and nearly forgotten, we were stunned by both the range of the collection and the extraordinary freshness of the works.

A pastel counterproof is made by placing a dampened sheet of paper on top of a pastel and applying pressure (by rubbing or by the use of a press) to transfer some of the surface of the pastel to the new sheet. The technique can be remarkably successful in creating a second work, which is in mirror image and is somewhat softer looking, while the pastel itself appears essentially unchanged, even if more than one counterproof impression was made from it.

This process was used frequently by artists of the eighteenth century but lapsed early in the nineteenth with the ascendancy of Romanticism, which demanded the weightier aesthetic of oil paint. In the later nineteenth century, the fresh and airy hues of pastel were once again found to be particularly appealing, and the flattened surfaces and subtle colors that result from the counterproof process naturally attracted artists who were immersed in the ethereal symbolism and patterns that characterized much Post-Impressionist art at the turn of the century.

Mary Cassatt's friend and champion, Edgar Degas, produced a great number of counterproofs of charcoal drawings and pastels, several of which he eventually reworked.* But Cassatt, who we now know produced a comparable body of work in this medium, appears to have left her counterproofs untouched.

Warren Adelson, in his Foreword, and Jay E. Cantor and Pamela A. Ivinski, in their essays, discuss the lively role of Ambroise Vollard as a motivating dealer in the artistic community of Paris of his time and examine Cassatt's counterproofs within the context of this moment. Without Vollard's interest, encouragement, and his ever hopeful projects for the future, much artwork of his era would never have been produced. The exhibition for which this catalogue has been published is an occasion to celebrate both the revelation of previously unknown works by Mary Cassatt and the vision of Ambroise Vollard.

We are delighted to add to the literature on the artist with the production of this volume, *Art in a Mirror: The Counterproofs of Mary Cassatt*, as a complement to our earlier publication, *Mary Cassatt, Prints and Drawings from the Artist's Studio*, and are pleased to continue our long-standing collaboration with Adelson Galleries and its fine staff.

Marc Rosen and Susan Pinsky

* These are included in the sale catalogues of works from the Degas studio
  as "Impressions en couleur et en noir" and "Impressions rehaussées de couleurs."

Mary Cassatt

"Vollard is a genius in his line"

Writing in 1968 to Adelyn Breeskin, who was then preparing her seminal catalogue of the work of Mary Cassatt, the Parisian collector/dealer Henri Petiet recounted a little-known episode in the relationship between Cassatt and Ambroise Vollard (1867–1939).[1] According to Petiet, who had acquired a portion of Vollard's collection after the latter's death, Vollard had encouraged Cassatt in the taking of counterproofs from some of her pastels. Petiet suggests that these were done around 1900 as preparatory steps for an intended series of lithographs of Cassatt's works. While the counterproofs resulting from that collaboration—48 of which are exhibited here for the first time—may well have been planned as a part of such a project, they were probably begun somewhat later. It is likely that the making of these counterproofs continued over a number of years, as the pastels from which they were made date from approximately 1889 to 1913.[2] And while Petiet's suggestion of a planned series of lithographs is entirely possible, the counterproofs may have been considered by both artist and dealer as ends in themselves.

The counterproof project probably began sometime after 1905, when Vollard became closely involved in acquiring works from Cassatt and marketing them to a growing number of collectors.[3] In many ways, this was a critical moment for both parties. Vollard, in little more than a decade, had made himself an active and important force in the international art market. Cassatt, meanwhile, had reached maturity as an artist and was becoming restless with her aesthetic strategies and the way her market and reputation were being managed by Galeries Durand-Ruel of Paris, her longtime dealer. She felt, with some justification, that she was not being recognized in the pantheon of the founding generation of Impressionist artists, whose ranks she had formally joined in 1879, through the offices of Edgar Degas. Moreover, she worried that her dealer was marketing her work to a parochial American audience and not to their international clientele.[4] Initially, Cassatt offered Vollard older works and honored her contract with Durand-Ruel by reserving her current production for their gallery, but by 1905, she was selling Vollard recent works.[5] She invited him to choose freely from her studio, and he responded by acquiring numerous works in all mediums. While she seems to have given her most highly finished paintings and pastels to Durand-Ruel for sale, Vollard's taste and interests were wide-ranging. Perhaps because of his own dedicated enthusiasm for both printmaking and book publishing and the complex stages involved in each process, he readily acquired less-finished compositions and multiple variations on specific subjects in pastels and drawings as well as working proofs and color variants of many of Cassatt's classic prints.[6]

Vollard first gained a toehold in the Impressionist market by befriending a number of Cassatt's contemporaries, including Renoir, Pissarro, and Degas.[7] These artists introduced Vollard to other artists and collectors, supplied him with their own works, and became collecting clients on occasion. The dealer had been active in the resale of Impressionist works from the establishment of his gallery in 1893, but he quickly moved into the marketing of artists associated with the newest aesthetic movement, Post-Impressionism, including Gauguin and Van Gogh. His 1895 exhibition and sale of the work of Paul Cézanne, the first accorded to that painter, confirmed Cézanne's position as a major artistic voice and earned Vollard plaudits as well. He simultaneously embraced the work of a number of younger artists, members of the group known as the Nabis, including Pierre Bonnard, Édouard Vuillard, Maurice Denis, and Ker-Xavier Roussel. In fact, Vollard's record of discovery and his active encouragement of new aesthetics in the work of diverse artists from Pablo Picasso and Henri Matisse to Maurice de Vlaminck and André Derain are legendary. He was noted also for his promotion of artists such as Odilon Redon, Georges Rouault, and Aristide Maillol, who pursued more personal styles, somewhat outside the dominant avant-garde trends of the period.[8]

Vollard's embrace of Cassatt in the early twentieth century is slightly puzzling in this context. She belonged to an older generation, although she had advanced beyond an Impressionist-influenced style to a bolder expression of modern life. Vollard seems to have been drawn to work of figural artists of the modern painting movement, and he made a specialty of offering pictures by Degas, Renoir, and Pissarro as well as their great precursor, Édouard Manet. Cassatt would have clearly fit within Vollard's canon, and he may even have heard rumors of her dissatisfaction with Durand-Ruel, as he regularly dined with and entertained a diverse group of artists and collectors and conducted what might be considered a salon in the small cellar dining room of his gallery on the Rue Lafitte.[9] Cassatt described the situation in a letter to Louisine Havemeyer, referring to Durand-Ruel's relationship with Degas: "He would not buy the things from Degas that Vollard gladly took and sold again at large profits. Vollard is a genius in his line he seems to be able to sell *anything*."[10] Cassatt had actually encountered Vollard as early as 1896 when she bought a Cézanne still life for her own collection, and by 1901, she had introduced him to her friends Henry O. and Louisine Havemeyer, who were to assemble a landmark collection of modern French painting. This led to a continuing relationship between Cassatt and Vollard, as she increasingly worked with the Havemeyers in enriching their collections, acting as an adviser and agent. (Part of her concern about Durand-Ruel was possibly the suspicion that they were using her to get closer to the Havemeyers and were not as dedicated to the promotion of her art as she had hoped.)

Something else about Cassatt would have earned Vollard's admiration: her outstanding accomplishments in the print field set her well apart from most of her contemporaries. Vollard had developed an infatuation with prints in the earliest years of his residence in Paris, which had become his home after he left the French island of La Réunion, in the Indian Ocean. As a young law student, he haunted the stalls of book and print dealers along the Parisian streets and the quays of the Seine and made his first purchases there. The resale of a few humble sketches acquired in this way had launched his art-dealing career, and he quickly parlayed an instinct for the potential of the overlooked into a successful art enterprise. His entry into the Parisian art world coincided with a near frenzy of enthusiasm for printmaking.[11] Paris was plastered with brightly colored posters and flooded with new publications extolling the delights of color prints and the talent of the artists who produced them. A variety of magazines and group portfolios as well as collections of and individual prints by specific artists were promoted for their marriage of high art and popular taste. A pioneering publication by André Marty, *L'Estampe*

Fig. 1
Pierre Bonnard (1867–1947)
La Petite Blanchisseuse, 1895–1896
Color lithograph,
printed by Clot
and published by Vollard

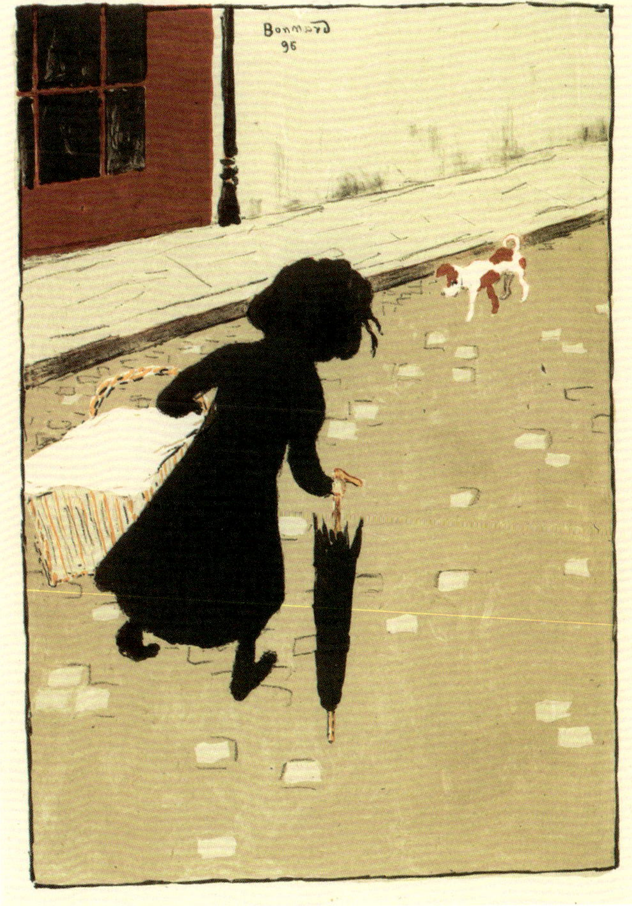

originale, published quarterly between 1893 and 1895, was succeeded by a host of similar ventures.

Ever alert to a marketing opportunity and possessed of a missionary energy, Vollard became, in turn, a publisher of print folios and, subsequently, of fine illustrated books. He entered this arena in 1895 with a portfolio of Bonnard lithographs, *Quelques aspects de la vie de Paris*, followed by the mixed portfolios: *L'Album des peintres-graveurs* (1896) and *L'Album d'estampes originales de la Galerie Vollard* (1897).

Like others in his circle, Vollard looked to painter-printmakers to explore and expand the aesthetic dimensions of the print medium beyond the merely reproductive and into the realm of original creation. He was especially drawn to color lithography, which, in contrast with etching and drypoint, allowed painters to approach the print medium in a spontaneous and painterly manner and facilitated the direct translation of their easel compositions into elegant print work. Working closely with the master printer August Clot, who had established his own shop around 1895, Vollard could produce print editions that involved the direct and detailed participation of the artists. Some, like Bonnard [Fig. 1] and Vuillard, assumed tight control of all stages in the development of the final print, seizing on the

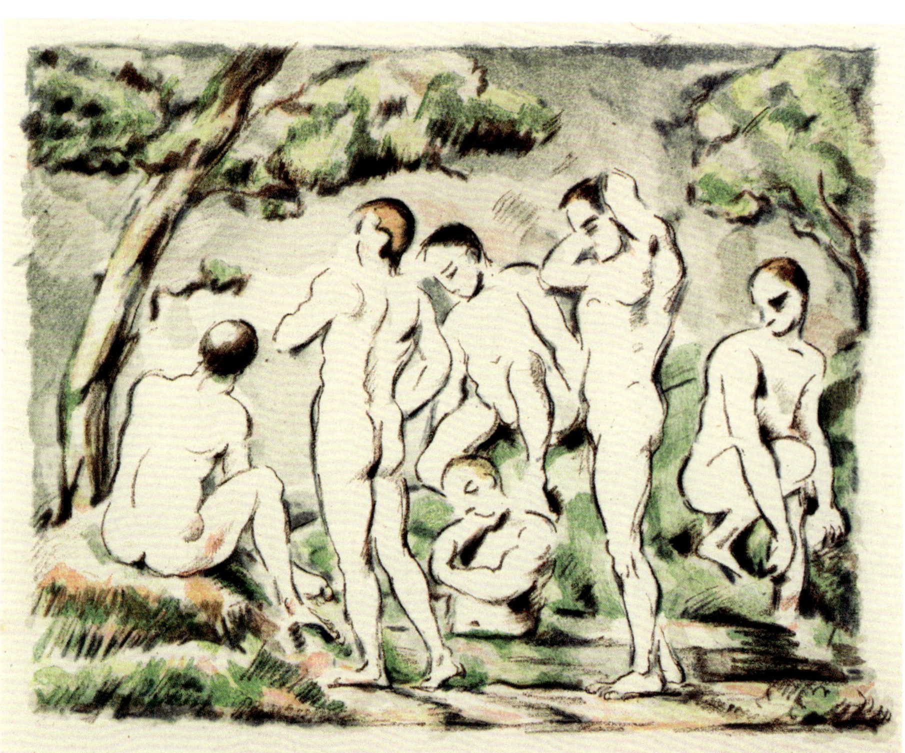

Fig. 2
Paul Cézanne (1839–1906)
Les Petits Baigneurs, 1897
Color lithograph,
printed by Clot
and published by Vollard

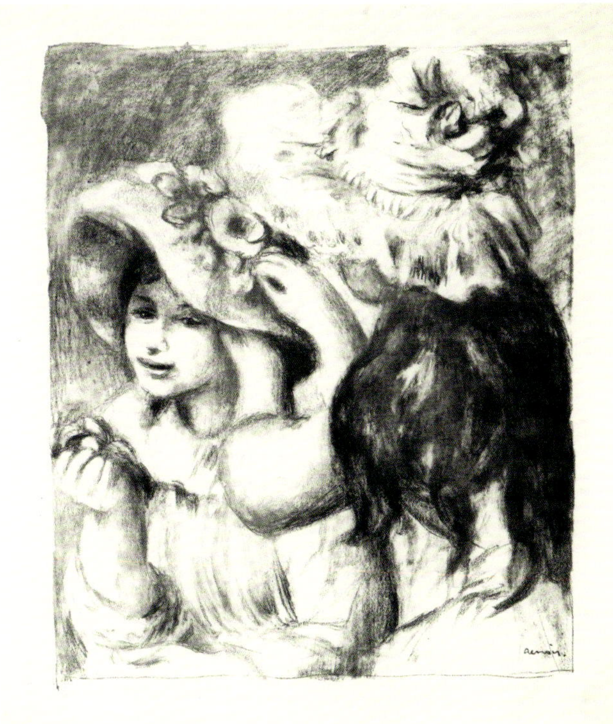 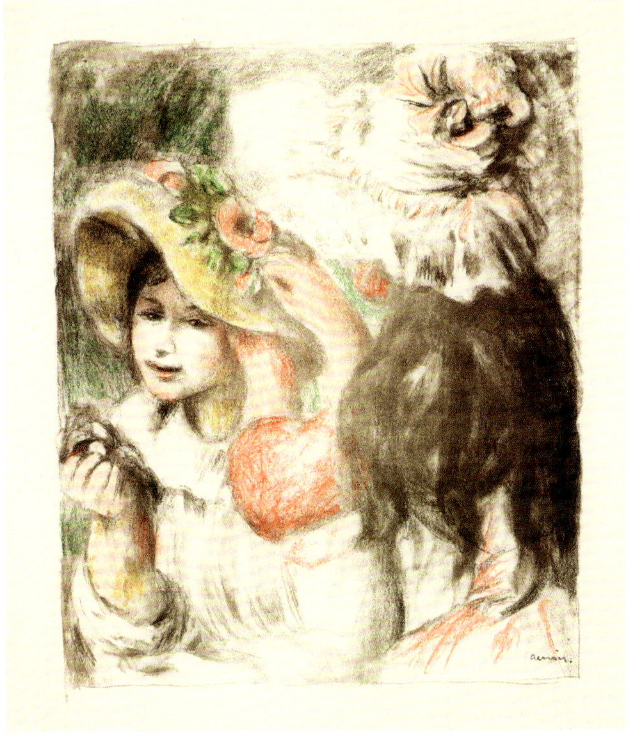

special aesthetic properties of the medium. But lithography also allowed painters to work at a distance, providing a drawing to be transferred to lithographic stone and then coloring printed proofs for transcription, one color at a time, to the separate stones needed to produce the completed color lithograph. For Cézanne, who built his watercolor compositions on a firmly drawn structure, this approach was ideal, and Clot was masterful in transcribing the areas of brushed color to be printed over the drawn base [Fig. 2]. Renoir for his part appreciated the freedom of working up his maquettes in pastel to be decomposed onto separate color stones by the skilled eye and hand of Clot [Figs. 3 and 4]. While critics battled to define the fine art print and separate it from mere reproductions, sophisticated printers like Clot often found themselves translating an artist's work, created in another medium, into a lithograph that would reflect the character and quality of the original medium. The result of such collaborations with Clot was a kind of artistic facsimile, not a dry or photomechanical replica, but a true evocation of the artist's vision and conception. While purists considered this type of work too removed from the particular qualities of the print medium, some, including Vollard, argued for the process as a desirable form of fine print production.[12]

Fig. 3 (above left)
Pierre-Auguste Renoir (1841–1919)
Chapeau épinglé, 2e planche,
ca. 1898
Lithograph,
printed by Clot
and published by Vollard

Fig. 4 (above right)
Pierre-Auguste Renoir (1841–1919)
Le Chapeau épinglé, 2e planche,
ca. 1898
Color lithograph,
printed by Clot
and published by Vollard

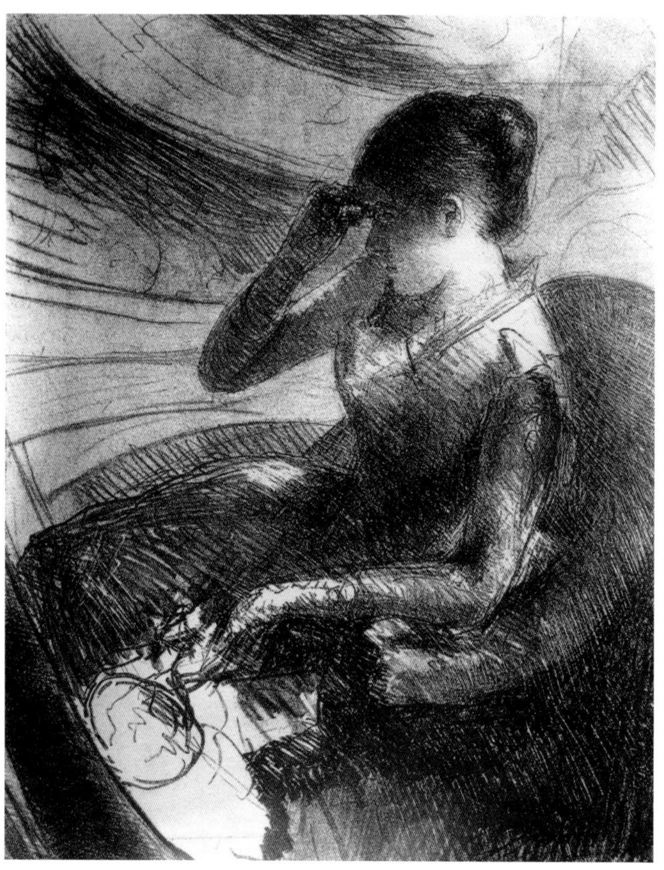

Fig. 5
Mary Cassatt (1844–1926)
Au Théâtre, ca. 1880
Lithograph

Most of Cassatt's own extensive printmaking experience had been in etching and drypoint.[13] At the beginning of her work as an etcher in 1879–1880, she produced a single lithograph, *Au Théâtre* [Fig. 5], but did not return to this medium for decades. Her print work was sporadic and carried out in campaigns of production that reached a crescendo with the great color prints of the early 1890s. Another burst of activity took place after the turn of the century, just at the moment when her relationship with Vollard was developing. It was also at this time that Cassatt produced her second lithograph, *Sara Wearing Her Bonnet and Coat* [Fig. 6], which has traditionally been dated to 1904 based on Breeskin's ascribed date of a related pastel.[14] (The counterproof that corresponds to this pastel is number 44 in this catalogue.)

Sara Wearing Her Bonnet and Coat is actually a transfer lithograph. Cassatt would have prepared the drawing on a piece of paper, and her design was then transferred to the lithographic stone, producing, in the final print, a duplicate of the original drawing. It is interesting to speculate that Vollard was the vehicle for the creation of this print, introducing Cassatt to the idea that she would have to do no more than provide an original work from which he would produce a print. This is precisely the procedure he followed with some other artists. Furthermore, Vollard would have been able to provide the connection with a lithographic printer. Cassatt's prior associations had been with printers of etchings. It would have been an easy segue from the production of this black-and-white lithograph to the suggestion of creating color lithographs based on her pastels.

On the surface, the sheer volume of her counterproofs might seem surprising (more than 130 are now recorded), but it is, in fact, quite consistent with Vollard's strategies of the period. Despite often lackluster print sales, he never stinted in the number of publications he undertook nor in the enormous ambition of individual projects. Deeply concerned with the quality of the final product, he chose artists, printers, paper, and type fonts with a connoisseur's eye. Many of his projects involved large numbers of prints that sometimes languished for decades in his shop until subsequent plates were produced or he focused again on the completion of the work.[15]

In spite of the protracted gestation and often unrealized ambition of his projects, artists continued to work with Vollard and considered him to be both a personal friend and a friend of their art. Cassatt seems to have willingly participated with both Durand-Ruel and Vollard in reaching out for new audiences, at times adjusting her work to suit that audience. Although she later complained that she had sold her soul to the dealers, she responded readily to their flattery as well as to requests for her works, which she released in increasing quantities, hoping that the broader exposure would help to secure her lasting reputation.[16] She also sold works out of pique with her relatives, to whom she had originally planned a large bequest. As her nieces and nephews matured and showed no real appreciation for art in general or hers in particular, Cassatt's earlier plans were abandoned, and she steadily raided her storerooms in search of material with which to supply the market.[17]

The opportunity to increase significantly the quantity of her work through the counterproof process was but one possible motive for the counterproof venture. Cassatt had long believed that printmaking, while a serious artistic pursuit appropriate for a modern painter, was also a healthy way of democratizing art and making it available to a broader audience.[18] It is possible that Vollard promised just such an opportunity with the creation of the counterproofs that could enlarge the size of her production and be offered less expensively than the pastels from which they were taken.

The counterproof process also fit within an experimental strategy that her friend and mentor Degas frequently explored. He often reworked his prints and monotypes, adding embellishments at times so extensive as to obliterate the underlying originals. The idea of improvising upon a given structure and pushing it in new and unexpected directions was one of the innovative notions of this period, which valued suggestive and individualized creations. Degas also produced counterproofs of his own pastels and drawings, which he

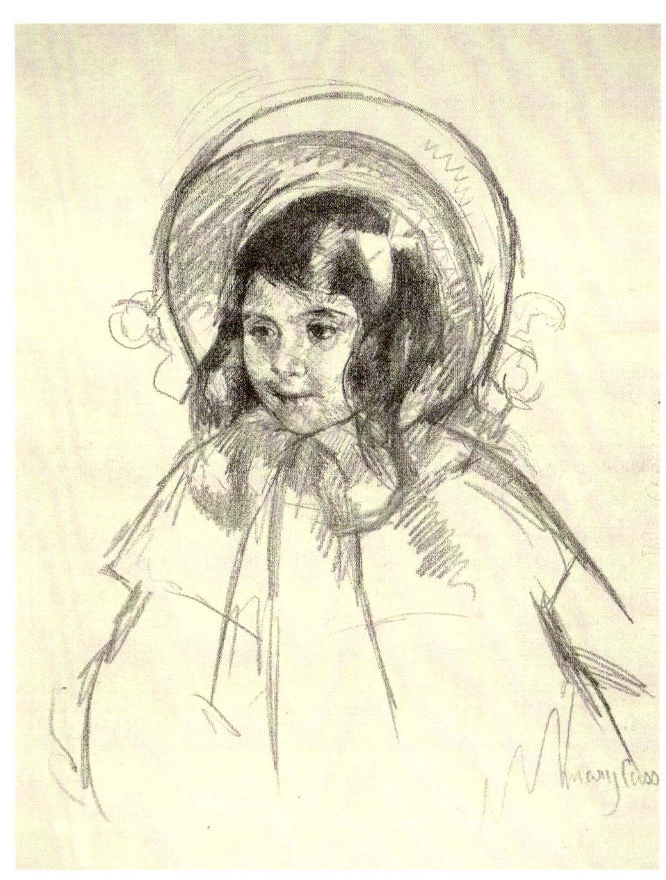

Fig. 6
Mary Cassatt (1844–1926)
Sara Wearing Her Bonnet and Coat, ca. 1904
Lithograph
(cf. BrCR 454 and cat. 44)

sometimes reworked in chalk and pastel.[19] Cassatt, long accustomed to a close collaboration with a printer during the production of her color prints a decade earlier, probably found comfort in a working relationship with Clot. Pulling the counterproofs also required the use of a lithographic press rather than an etching press such as that owned by Cassatt.

Like Degas's reverse impressions of his drawings and pastels, the Cassatt counterproofs offered an occasion for innovative reworking. Since the image was reversed, it became, in effect, an entirely different and original work to be confronted on its own terms. Of course, Cassatt would have been free at any time to return to an older and sometimes "unfinished" pastel and carry it forward. However, she generally seems to have stopped working on a pastel because she had gone as far as she cared to with it.[20] The occasion to start afresh on a new picture, sometimes of the same subject or of a related image, preempted the constant reworking of older pieces. The counterproof, on the other hand, was essentially a new work, and if these were intended to be the springboard to variations, they would have provided an exciting opportunity. At present, there is no clear evidence of the degree to which these counter-proofs may have been used in this way. Since they remained in Vollard's hands, it seems likely that this was yet another of his grand but unrealized schemes.

There is also another tempting explanation for the quantity of counter-proofs. It is possible that Vollard, who had regularly published volumes that aimed at promoting the work of artists he favored, intended to use the coun-terproofs in the production of a folio of Cassatt's work in pastel.[21] As reversed images, the counterproofs would have provided an easy template for transfer-ring the pastel image to the lithographic stone. And Clot was noted for his technical skill in translating images to retain the character of the original. Furthermore, the fact that the pastels from which these counterproofs were taken range over several decades of the artist's work could support this specu-lation, but sadly, the only documentary evidence currently known is the letter from Petiet to Breeskin, written decades after the counterproofs were made.

As they are, the counterproofs remain striking images, very much in line with the aesthetic promulgated by artists of the Vollard circle in the later nine-teenth and early twentieth centuries. Their soft tonal qualities and suggestive modulations of color relate these works to images by a host of contemporary modern painters, especially the Nabis, including Vuillard, Bonnard, and Denis, as well as those of a consummate pastellist like Odilon Redon. Cassatt's coun-terproofs share with their work a subtle, evocative, and personal expression.

The imagery is entirely her own but the aesthetic is that of the newer age of the early twentieth century. For lovers of the Symbolists and the Nabis (and Vollard was high in their ranks), these images would have found special favor. The lessons she had learned in her early activities, including her understanding of the organization of broad and simplified forms, the calculated adjustments of flat areas of color, and the thoughtful enhancements of lines and shapes, all of which lurked beneath the surface of her art in the last decade of the nineteenth century, become evident in these counterproofs. Whatever Cassatt and Vollard had in mind for them, the counterproofs provide the modern viewer with an exciting insight into an artist's creative energy and imagination that speaks over the many years since their creation.

Jay E. Cantor

NOTES

1. Unlocated letter from Henri Petiet, dated by Adelyn Breeskin as July 21, 1968, and excerpted by her in letters to Una E. Johnson (July 11, 1977) and Riva Castleman, Curator of Prints and Illustrated Books, The Museum of Modern Art (June 20, 1977), in the files of the Mary Cassatt Catalogue Raisonné Committee.

2. There is no precise indication of the sequence in which the pastels were acquired by Vollard or when the counterproof project was begun, but it seems likely that it commenced fairly soon after Vollard began his extensive dealings with Cassatt ca. 1905–1906, since she appears to have been in an ambitious stage of work at this moment. The counterproof project must have been begun before late 1908, when the pastel from which the counterproof *Head of Margot Looking to Right* (see cat. 45) was acquired by an American collector. The latest pastel of which there is a known counterproof was executed ca. 1913 (see cat. 5).

3. Una E. Johnson, *Ambroise Vollard, Editeur: Prints, Books, Bronzes* (New York: The Museum of Modern Art, 1977); and Douglas Druick, "Cezanne's Lithographs," *The National Gallery of Canada Bulletin* 19 (1972), pp. 119–37, provide a good overview of Vollard's extensive publishing projects as well as his complex relationships with the artists in his circle.

4. Nancy Mowll Mathews, in *Mary Cassatt: A Life* (New York: Villard Books, 1994), traces Cassatt's artistic ambitions and her interaction with dealers, collectors, and the marketplace over the course of her lifetime.

5. Kevin Sharp, "How Mary Cassatt Became an American Artist," in *Mary Cassatt: Modern Woman*, ed. Judith A. Barter (Chicago: The Art Institute of Chicago in association with Harry N. Abrams, New York, 1998), pp. 162–4. Although Cassatt had a handful of transactions with Vollard prior to 1905, by that time it appears she invited him to choose more liberally from her works.

6. *Mary Cassatt, Prints and Drawings from the Artist's Studio* (Princeton, N.J.: Princeton University Press, 2000) provides a study of Cassatt's prints and drawings and documents the range of prints and drawings that survived as a group from Vollard's collection until their dispersal through Adelson Galleries in the exhibition for which this publication served as the catalogue.

7. Ambroise Vollard, *Recollections of a Picture Dealer* (New York: Dover Books, 2002), translated by Violet M. MacDonald and first published in English by Little, Brown & Company, Boston, in 1936.

8. Johnson, *Ambroise Vollard*, pp. 17–9, 127–71.

9. Vollard, *Recollections of a Picture Dealer*, pp. 81–98. This chapter, entitled "The Cellar," provides insight into the range of conversation that occurred at these meals. Glimpses of Vollard's working methods and complex relationships with collectors and artists are provided throughout this volume. He recounts numerous instances of how a casual remark led him to important discoveries.

10. Mary Cassatt to Louisine Havemeyer, Dec. 4, [1913], in *Cassatt and Her Circle, Selected Letters*, ed. Nancy Mowll Mathews (New York: Abbeville Press, 1984), p. 313. See also Frances Weitzenhoffer, *The Havemeyers: Impressionism Comes to America* (New York: Harry N. Abrams, 1986) for a discussion of the relationships between Cassatt, the Havemeyers, and Vollard.

11. Phillip Dennis Cate and Sinclair Hamilton Hitchings, *The Color Revolution, Color Lithography in France, 1890–1900* (Santa Barbara, CA and Salt Lake City, UT: Peregrine Smith, 1978) surveys the developments in printmaking, publishing, and critical reception during this period. See also John Ittman, *Post-Impressionist Prints: Paris in the 1890's* (Philadelphia: Philadelphia Museum of Art, 1998), and Phillip Dennis Cate, Gale B. Murray, and Richard Thomson, *Prints Abound: Paris in the 1890s: From the Collections of Virginia and Ira Jackson and the National Gallery of Art* (Washington, D.C.: National Gallery of Art, 2001), and Colta Ives, "An Art for Everyday," in *Pierre Bonnard, The Graphic Art* (New York: The Metropolitan Museum of Art and Harry N. Abrams, 1989), pp. 3–38.

12. Druick, *Cézanne's Lithographs*, pp. 119–22, discusses Vollard's commitment to lithography, the commercial opportunities he explored, and his collaboration with Clot in producing prints both with and without close involvement of the artist, as well as some of the critical reactions to his print activities. See also Pat Gilmour, "Cher Monsieur Clot, Auguste Clot and his role as a colour lithographer," in *Lasting Impressions, Lithography as Art* (Canberra: Australian National Gallery, 1988) pp. 129–75.

13. Nancy Mowll Mathews and Barbara Stern Shapiro, *Mary Cassatt: The Color Prints* (Washington, D.C.: National Gallery of Art, 1989) and Adelyn Dohme Breeskin, *Mary Cassatt: A Catalogue Raisonné of the Graphic Work* (Washington, D.C.: Smithsonian Institution Press, 1979).

14. This pastel is currently dated ca. 1901–1904 by the Mary Cassatt Catalogue Raisonné Committee.

15. See Johnson, *Ambroise Vollard*, pp. 27–29 and 32–40, for the range and extent of Vollard's prints, and bronzes. Johnson lists 244 titles in her catalogue raisonné of Vollard's publications, some of which were albums or books containing numerous individual prints. In addition to the projects that Vollard completed, a number of his planned publications were produced after his death by other publishers. See Gilmour, "Cher Monsieur Clot," p. 143.

16. Anna Louise Thorne, "My Afternoon with Mary Cassatt," *School Arts* 59 (May 1960), p. 12.

17. Mathews, *Mary Cassatt: A Life*, pp. 309–310. Cassatt's disfavor also resulted from her disappointment at her family's attitudes toward feminist causes, particularly universal suffrage, which she supported.

18. Mathews, *Mary Cassatt: A Life*, p. 234.

19. *Edgar Degas, Defining the Modernist Edge*, ed. Jennifer Gross (New Haven and London: Yale University Press, 2003). See also *Degas's Atelier at Auction, Paintings, Pastels & Drawings*, Vol. l, Sales I & II, 1918, and Vol. 2, Sales III & IV, 1919 (San Francisco: Alan Wofsy Fine Arts, 1989) for an inventory of Degas's extensive counterproof activity.

20. Jay E. Cantor, "Mary Cassatt: Drawing on Drawing," in *Mary Cassatt, Prints and Drawings from the Artist's Studio*, pp. 127–33.

21. Gilmour, "Cher Monsieur Clot," pp. 166, 169, describes Clot's lithographic experiments after the turn of the twentieth century and his response to the softening of the demand for prints. Petiet, in his correspondence with Breeskin, makes the intriguing suggestion that Vollard undertook a counterproof/lithographic project with Cassatt at Clot's suggestion. See also Harriet K. Stratis, "Innovation and Tradition in Mary Cassatt's Pastels, A Study of Her Methods and Materials," in *Mary Cassatt: Modern Woman*, pp. 221–2.

After Impressionism: Cassatt's Counterproofs and Her Later Career

Mary Cassatt is best known as an Impressionist, one of the renegade artists who rejected the moribund aesthetic conventions of the 1870s in favor of spontaneous brushwork, radiant color, and modern-life subject matter. To call her an Impressionist is to situate her work quickly and effectively within the continuum of art history. Yet, this label also does Cassatt a disservice, for it fails to acknowledge that she continued to experiment and respond to new artistic currents throughout her career, which extended until the mid-1910s. The 48 pictures featured in this catalogue and on view in the exhibition *Art in a Mirror: The Counterproofs of Mary Cassatt*, all of them reverse impressions made from pastels dating from approximately 1889 to 1913, open a window onto a little-studied artmaking technique and attest to this artist's continuing innovation and originality long after the dissolution of the Impressionist group in 1886. Furthermore, these counterproofs provide a wealth of new information about Cassatt's palette because many of the pastels from which they were made have never been published in color, and seven examples represent previously unknown compositions, having been made from unrecorded pastels.

A counterproof is created by placing a moistened sheet of blank paper over an artwork such as a recently pulled etching or a charcoal drawing, and applying pressure, usually by running the papers through a printing press. The pressure causes a reversed image of the original to be transferred to the blank sheet. Until recently, fewer than 22 pastels by Cassatt were known to have had counterproofs made from them. With the discovery of the collection from which the current exhibition is drawn, we now know that counterproofs were made from at least 67 pastels, and more than 130 impressions have been catalogued to date.

In general, Cassatt's pastel counterproofs are characterized by a delicately flattened surface and softly luminous colors that echo certain aspects of the "Symbolist" or "Idealist" aesthetic that had begun to emerge by the final

Note: Numbers in brackets refer to catalogue numbers.

Impressionist exhibition. Whereas the Impressionists had been greatly concerned to depict subjects drawn from nature and modern life, many artists of the Post-Impressionist era sought to illustrate otherworldly scenes and subjective states of mind by means of symbols and emotionally expressive rather than realistic colors and lines. Many of Cassatt's counterproofs are distinguished by an ethereal beauty equal to that found in works considered to be exemplars of Symbolism, such as Odilon Redon's 1885 pastel *Béatrice* (private collection), and his 1896–1897 color lithograph of the same subject [Fig. 1]. That the Cassatt pastels selected for counterproofing evince Symbolist qualities may also reflect the taste of the dealer and publisher Ambroise Vollard, at whose behest the counterproofs were made, for he commissioned not only the *Béatrice* lithograph but also many of the greatest Post-Impressionist color prints.[1]

The first significant artistic endeavor completed by Cassatt after the Impressionists disbanded was a series of drypoint etchings that she exhibited with a new society of artists, the *Peintres-Graveurs* (Painter-Printmakers), in 1890. While these skillfully drawn prints represent a high point of her incisive realism, the artist at this moment was not limited to any particular medium or style. Beginning around 1890, she began to employ the same cast of models in images done in a range of stylistic inflections and an assortment of mediums, which she carried to varying degrees of finish. For instance, the moonfaced child who appears in *Hélène of Septeuil* [Fig. 2], a drypoint from the series mentioned above, is also found in a highly finished pastel titled *Hélène of Septeuil* (William Benton Museum of Art, University of Connecticut, Storrs), as well as in a loosely executed oil sketch, *Hélène Is Restless* (Portland Museum of Art, Maine), and in the pastel of the earliest date after which a counterproof is known, *Hélène of Septeuil, with a Parrot* (last known in a private collection), ca. 1889–1890 (see cat. 30).

While the drypoint *Hélène of Septeuil* [Fig. 2] epito-
mizes Cassatt's probing realism, achieved with an econ-
omy of line, the Storrs pastel demonstrates a Symbolist
interest in compressed space and the abstract play of patterns while also incorporating a reference to Madonna and
Child imagery by using the broad-brimmed hat to suggest
a halo. With the advent of Post-Impressionism, images from
the history of Western art once again became suitable
inspiration for artists searching to develop a universal
aesthetic language and to explore themes of enduring
import. Religious subjects such as the Madonna and Child
were no longer taboo for the modernist artist, as they had
been during the Impressionist era. Cassatt, who had
devoted herself to the study of old master works for the
first ten years she lived in Europe, integrated elements
derived from traditional sacred imagery into her mother-
and-child subjects with greater frequency beginning in the
late 1880s. Yet, she intended no overtly spiritual message in
these pictures, and they were perceived by patrons and
critics (especially those in the United States) as glorifying
the healthy child as the most important figure in the "religion of humanity."[2]

After 1886, Cassatt also increasingly turned to secular and genre scenes by
the old masters as sources to be translated into her own modernist vision.
The counterproof *Hélène of Septeuil, with a Parrot* [30], representing the same
girl seen in the drypoint [Fig. 2] and the Storrs pastel, looks back to another
tradition, that of seventeenth-century Dutch and Flemish portraiture, which
often posed children with pet birds.[3] (The parrot in particular symbolized
the docility and discipline necessary for the child's education.) With its velvety
surface and soft yet vibrant colors, however, the mood of the counterproof
Hélène of Septeuil, with a Parrot is almost dreamlike, in keeping with the
Symbolist aesthetic, and quite unlike the realism of either Cassatt's own
drypoints or pictures in the Northern European tradition.

The inclination toward Symbolism evident in Cassatt's works of the late
1880s and early 1890s was fostered by a commission to paint a mural for the
1893 World's Columbian Exposition on the theme of "Modern Woman."[4]
Cassatt's allegorical conception for the project, which she described as "Young
women plucking the fruits of knowledge or science," involved three painted

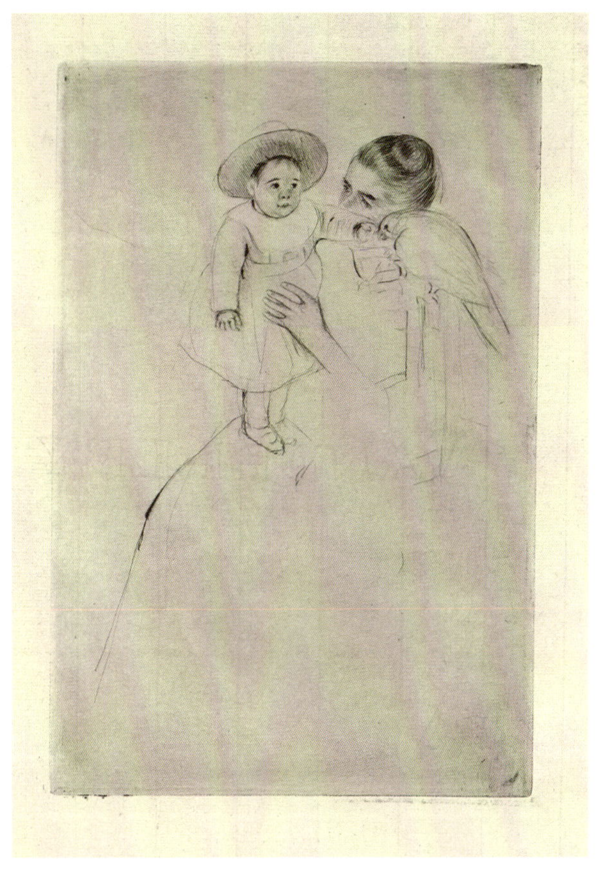

Fig. 2
Mary Cassatt
*Hélène of Septeuil [Enfant au
Perroquet]*, 1889–1890
Drypoint

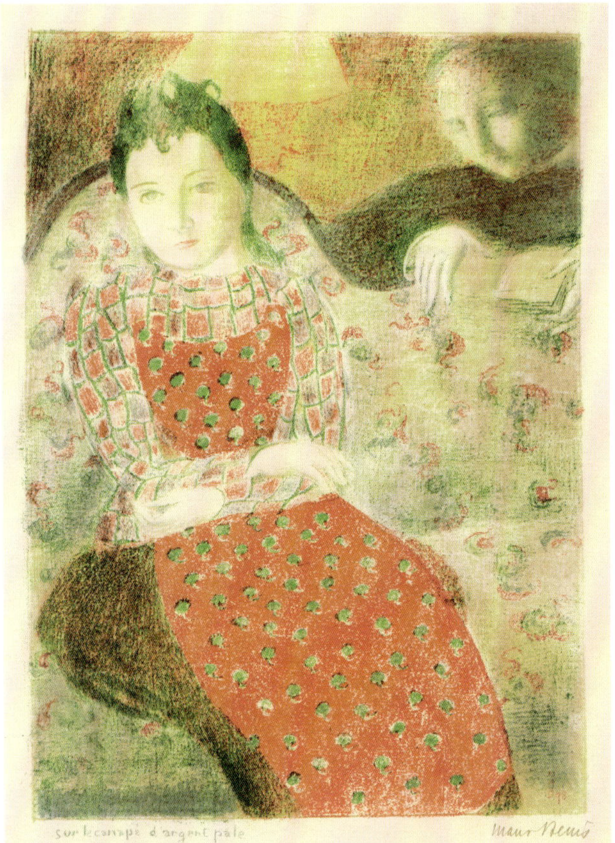

Fig. 3
Maurice Denis (1870–1943)
Sur le Canapé d'argent pâle, 1898
Color lithograph,
printed by Clot
and published by Vollard

panels.[5] A central section representing women and girls harvesting fruit in an orchard was flanked by two smaller panels, one showing girls chasing a figure who symbolized fame, and the other depicting women participating in the arts of dance and music. The mural's program supplied the artist with a rich vein of imagery that she explored through the mid-1890s in works including *Woman and Child in Front of a Fruit Tree* [24], a delicate counterproof after an undocumented pastel that also closely relates to a significant oil painting, *Baby Reaching for an Apple* of 1893 (The Virginia Museum of Fine Arts, Richmond). Another mother-and-child counterproof from this period, *Sketch of a Mother Looking Down at Thomas* [11], belongs to a group of works created circa 1894 that were interpreted by a critic of the time as embodying "the wonderful, infinitely motherly yearning over the queer, little unresponsive being of which she knows so little."[6]

The "Modern Woman" theme that Cassatt treated in the 1893 Columbian Exposition mural also spurred her to create a number of compelling images of women and older girls in the mid-1890s. Expanding upon the theme of women cooperating in the pursuit of knowledge and the arts, Cassatt depicted a woman playing the banjo while a girl leans affectionately upon her shoulders, as seen in the counterproof, *The Banjo Lesson* [2]. This image, with its reference to Japanese woodcuts of women playing the samisen, a banjo-like instrument, also underscores the importance of non-Western sources, including Persian miniatures, for Cassatt's aesthetic of the period.

Like *The Banjo Lesson*, many of her pictures from the mid-1890s utilize profile or near-profile poses, among them *Young Woman Reflecting* [35] and *Madame and Her Maid* [8]. Feminist scholars have traced this convention to fifteenth-century Florence, where it was used as a means of displaying the female visage for scrutiny by the possessive male gaze.[7] By the late nineteenth century, and in Cassatt's hands, the profile pose (which may also have been derived from ancient Greek and Egyptian bas reliefs) instead functions to imply that these women are inaccessible, for they are engrossed in their private thoughts and activities. The atmosphere of quiet concentration or reverie in these pictures shows the artist to be working within the same aesthetic current as other Symbolists of the period, such as Redon and the Nabi artist Maurice Denis in their respective color lithographs, *Béatrice* [Fig. 1], of 1896–1897, and *Sur le Canapé d'argent pâle* [Fig. 3], of 1898. Even Cassatt's *Portrait of a Young Woman in Green* [4], which makes use of a three-quarter pose and was done in conjunction with a formal commission, exhibits a comparable air of contemplative reserve.[8]

If Cassatt often favored profile poses when depicting women in the 1890s, in the same period she also created many maternal images in which the mother's face is nearly or even completely obscured. While utilizing a profile view in the charming image *A Kiss for Baby Anne (No. 1)* [3], she turned the mother's head away from the spectator in the similarly composed *Mother Louise Holding up Her Blue-Eyed Child* [32]. Nevertheless, the strength of the mother-child bond in the latter work is in no way diminished. Rather, as with the pictures of women discussed above, the mood is one of intense absorption. In *Baby Charles Looking Over His Mother's Shoulder (No. 2)* [22], the mother's profile is lost behind the head and shoulder of the child. Attention is consequently shifted to the adorable baby and to the formal aspects of the work's color and pattern. The resulting tension between anecdote and decorative effects again shows Cassatt to be in congruence with advanced Symbolist ideas, as seen in works such as Édouard Vuillard's ca. 1899 color lithograph, *Sur le Pont de l'Europe* [Fig. 4].

At the turn of the century, Cassatt increasingly focused her work on a small group of models. One figure, a sweet-faced brunette who has traditionally been identified as Margot Lux, appears in numerous pictures beginning around 1898 or 1899. Though the name Margot is most commonly associated with pictures of a slightly later date, such as *Study of Margot in a Fluffy Hat* [25], it seems possible, given the resemblance, that she is also the infant portrayed in counterproofs including *Baby Embracing Her Mother* [34], *Sketch of Woman in Light Green Wrapper Holding Her Child* [48], *Nude Dark-Eyed Little Girl with Mother in Patterned Wrapper* [31], and in the image now known as *Nicolle and Her Mother* [23].

At this same moment Cassatt also began to draw upon old master Madonna and Child sources with even greater frequency than in the early 1890s. These pictures of the infant Margot recall a compositional template established by Raphael in Renaissance icons including the *Small Cowper Madonna* (National Gallery of Art, Washington, D.C.), which grew in popularity after being extolled

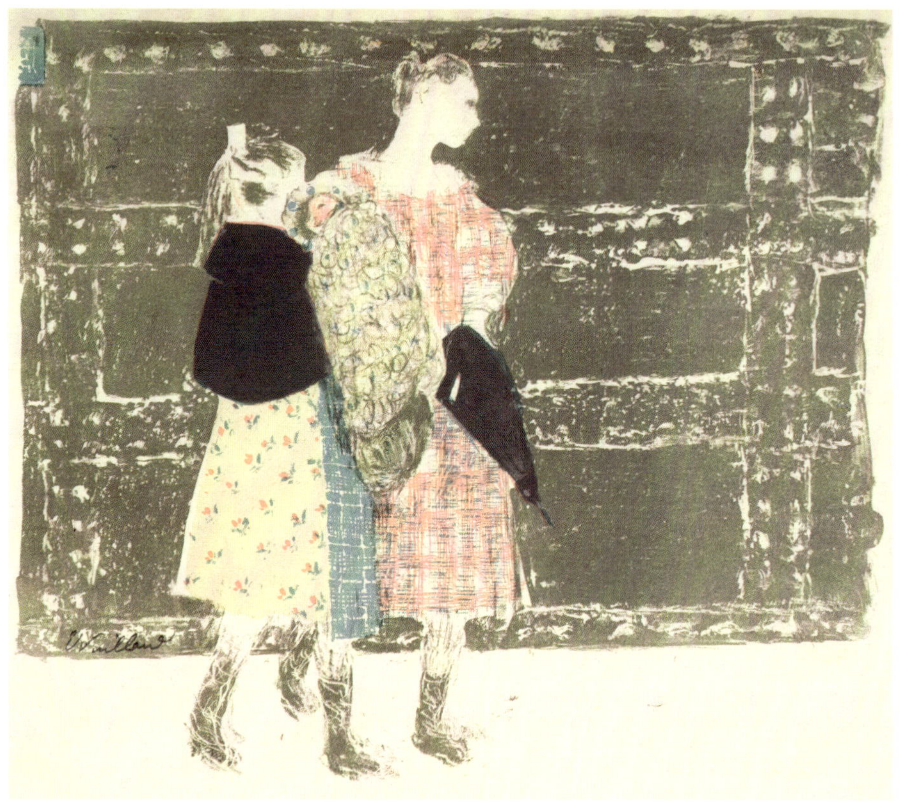

as "perhaps the most lovely of all Raphael's Madonnas" by the eminent connoisseur Giovanni Morelli in 1883.[9] In the case of the counterproofs, their Raphaelesque aspects were only accentuated by the slight blurring inherent to the process, which resulted in an effect akin to Raphael's celebrated *sfumato*.[10] The counterproof of *Nude Dark-Eyed Little Girl with Mother in Patterned Wrapper* [31] in particular displays this attractive quality.

A slightly older Margot is featured alone in quite a few pictures done in the years around 1900. In a rather elaborate composition, *Margot in a Dark Red Costume Seated on a Round-Backed Chair* [7], she is posed, as Cassatt's girls often are, upon a chair that resembles a throne. Other works, among them *Head of Margot Looking to Right* [45], *Margot Wearing a Blue Gauze Bonnet* [6], *Margot in a Pale Rose Hat* [28 and 29], and *Bust Length Sketch of Margot in a Big Hat and a Red Dress* [20], spotlight the child's face framed by an assortment of showy chapeaux. One especially lovely example of this type, *Margot in a Bonnet* [14], is one of those counterproofs that provides our only evidence of an unrecorded pastel. Cassatt also adorned a blond model with a similar accessory in pictures including the counterproof *Head of Simone in a Green Bonnet with Wavy Brim (No. 2)* [18].

The older Margot appears again with a woman posing as her mother or nurse (traditionally identified as the model Reine Lefebvre) in a number of works done around the turn of the century, some studies for which were used to make reverse impressions. These images, however, are less dependent upon the Madonna and Child model than those in which Margot appears as an infant. The counterproofs *Heads of Reine and of Margot* [26] and *Study of Margot in a Fluffy Hat* [25], for example, in which the child leans upon an elbow placed on the woman's knee, resemble Netherlandish compositions while also featuring modern-day elements such as fashionable dresses and hats.[11] The girl portrayed in the counterproof *Sara Wearing a Bonnet and Coat* [44] and in the closely related pastel, *Sara in a Green Coat* (The Metropolitan Museum of Art, New York), may actually represent Margot a bit older than she was in works such as *Heads of Reine and of Margot*, or these pictures may represent another dark-haired girl entirely.

Cassatt also created numerous images depicting blond girls in the early years of the twentieth century. Though they are usually identified as either "Sara" or "Simone," it is often quite difficult to specify which girl is which with complete confidence. Two of the earliest images of these blond models can be seen in the counterproofs *Study of Sara* [40] and *Simone in a Round-Backed Upholstered Chair* [10], while *Simone in a White Bonnet Seated with Clasped Hands (No. 1)* [41] may also represent the same child.

Unlike Margot, whom Cassatt most often depicted alone or in the company of an adult woman, the artist frequently portrayed her blond girls either with small dogs or in multifigure compositions. In most cases, the girls wear fanciful hats and hair ribbons, again bringing to mind seventeenth-century Dutch portrait conventions updated in accordance with modern fashions in accessories and pet-keeping.[12] It also appears that these "Sara with dog" compositions were favored by Vollard, because Cassatt's primary dealer, Galeries Durand-Ruel, acquired very few of them.

Counterproofs in which "Sara" appears with a canine companion include *Sara in a Dark Bonnet Holding Her Dog* [17], *Sara Looking Down at a Dog* [43], *Sara, in a Bonnet with Streamers Loose, and Her Dog* [42], and *Smiling Sara in a Big Hat Holding Her Dog (No. 1)* [12]. Especially notable among these images are *Sara in a Large Flowered Hat, Looking Right, Holding Her Dog* [13], which displays an unusually detailed interior for Cassatt's work of this period, and *Sara and Her Dog* [15], a reverse impression pulled from a pastel that has only recently emerged. Another counterproof, *Girl Wearing a Hat with a Blue Bow* [16], was made from an unrecorded study for a similar picture from this era.

Girl in a Hat with a Black Ribbon [19] (also a counterproof of an unrecorded pastel) relates to a group of works from around 1901–1902 in which a round-faced blond model is posed with a mother or nurse. In *Simone Seated on the Grass Next to Her Mother* [9], the dark lines of the ribbon on the girl's hat and the woman's dress serve to anchor the amorphous patterns of their dresses and the flowering landscape behind them. Another counterproof from this period, *Mother Combing Sara's Hair (No. 2)* [1], places the same figures within a more intimate domestic setting, inspired by seventeenth-century Dutch and Flemish pictures of women grooming their children. Yet the work is simultaneously quite modern, for it flattens space, employs flat blocks of bright color, and presents the mother's back to the viewer.

Old master precedents also inform pictures from the turn of the century that exemplify Cassatt's "Modern Madonna" imagery.[13] The counterproof *Reine Lefebvre with Blond Baby and Sara Holding a Cat* [21], for instance, translates Renaissance religious icons such as Raphael's *Garvagh Madonna* (National Gallery, London) into a contemporary idiom with the addition of fashionable clothing and a pet cat. This particular counterproof testifies to the significant role that Vollard played in Cassatt's life in the 1900s, for it displays a reverse inscription that reads "à Mons[ieur] Vollard / avec mes compliments [...] / Mary Cassatt." *Mother Holding Red-Haired Child* [39], a counterproof after an unrecorded pastel, focuses on the maternal dyad, as does *Mother Jeanne Embracing Her Baby* [38], a reverse impression of a pastel associated with one of Cassatt's most beloved "Modern Madonna" pictures, *The Caress* (Smithsonian American Art Museum, Washington, D.C.).

In addition to the young girls identified as Margot, Sara, and Simone, who served as Cassatt's models for many works in the years around 1900, Cassatt later portrayed a number of slightly older, dark-haired subjects, including the girls now known as Françoise and Adele. The latter appears in two similar counterproofs likely dating around 1908–1909, *Head of Adele (No. 3)* [47] and *Head of Adele (No. 4)* [46]. At this time Cassatt also returned to the subject of nursing, which she had first explored in the drypoint series of 1889–1890. The counterproofs *Mother Jeanne Nursing Her Child (Profile Left) (No. 3)* [36], *Mother Rose Nursing Her Child* [33], and *Mother and Child* [37] all relate to an oil painting now in the Art Institute of Chicago, *Mother Nursing Her Baby*, ca. 1908. Cassatt also continued to create sensitive depictions of the mother-child bond in pastels from her late career, including *Baby John on His Mother's Lap* [27], ca. 1908–1910, and *Child Leaning Against Her Young Mother* [5], ca. 1913.

The works featured in *Art in a Mirror: The Counterproofs of Mary Cassatt* readily demonstrate that the artist continued to innovate and to create appealing images long after her Impressionist days had ended. The seven counterproof images made after unrecorded pastels are complete revelations [14, 16, 19, 24, 28/29, 34, and 39], expanding our knowledge of her pastel production.[14] Others teach us something new about related works that are known only in black-and-white reproductions. For example, the now unlocated pastel from which the counterproof *Baby Charles Looking Over His Mother's Shoulder (No. 2)* [22] was made, while perfectly lovely in a black-and-white reproduction in the Breeskin catalogue raisonné, is discovered to be a nuanced exercise in color and pattern. And still others, including *Sara, in a Bonnet with Streamers Loose, and Her Dog* [42], *Madame and Her Maid* [8], and *Nude Dark-Eyed Little Girl with Mother in Patterned Wrapper* [31], confirm that Cassatt was an original master in depicting her signature subjects: young girls, modern women, and maternity.

Pamela A. Ivinski

NOTES

1. Una E. Johnson's *Ambroise Vollard, Éditeur: Prints, Books, Bronzes* (New York: The Museum of Modern Art, 1977) treats the subject of Vollard's career as a print publisher. For more information on Cassatt's counterproofs in the context of late nineteenth-century printmaking and the artists of Vollard's circle, see the essay by Jay E. Cantor in this same volume, "Vollard is a genius in his line," as well as my article, "The Pastel Counterproofs of Mary Cassatt," in *The Magazine Antiques* 166 (November 2004), pp. 144–53. For a broader view of Cassatt's career as a printmaker, see Nancy Mowll Mathews and Barbara Stern Shapiro, *Mary Cassatt: The Color Prints* (Washington, D.C.: National Gallery of Art, 1989), as well as Adelyn Dohme Breeskin, *Mary Cassatt: A Catalogue Raisonné of the Graphic Work* (Washington, D.C.: Smithsonian Institution Press, 1979).

2. For more on this topic, see Pamela A. Ivinski, *Mary Cassatt, the Maternal Body, and Modern Connoisseurship* (unpublished doctoral diss., City University of New York, 2003), Vol. I., pp. 469–72.

3. A number of beautiful Dutch paintings of this type are illustrated in the exhibition catalogue *Pride and Joy: Children's Portraits in the Netherlands, 1500–1700*, eds. Jan Baptist Bedaux and Rudi Ekkart (Ghent and Amsterdam: Ludion Press, distributed by Harry N. Abrams, New York, 2000). The child in the counterproof *Hélène of Septeuil, with a Parrot* [30] is dressed in a manner quite similar to the figure depicted in the painting *Unidentified Boy* (Rijksmuseum, Amsterdam), illustrated in *Pride and Joy* on p. 165.

4. Recent studies of Cassatt's mural include Sally Webster, *Eve's Daughter/Modern Woman: A Mural by Mary Cassatt* (Urbana: University of Illinois Press, 2004); Judith Barter, "Mary Cassatt: Themes, Sources, and the Modern Woman," in *Mary Cassatt: Modern Woman*, ed. Judith A. Barter (Chicago: The Art Institute of Chicago in association with Harry N. Abrams, New York, 1998), pp. 87–97; and Ivinski, *Mary Cassatt, the Maternal Body, and Modern Connoisseurship*, Vol. I, pp. 341–53.

5. Cassatt described the mural in a letter to Bertha Palmer, October 11 [1892], reprinted in *Cassatt and Her Circle: Selected Letters*, ed. Nancy Mowll Mathews (New York: Abbeville Press, 1984), p. 238.

6. William Walton, "Miss Mary Cassatt," *Scribner's Magazine* 19 (March 1896), p. 360. Walton was discussing the pastel *Mother Looking Down at Thomas* (Pushkin Museum of Fine Arts, Moscow). The pastel from which the counterproof *Sketch of a Mother Looking Down at Thomas* [11] was made is closely related to the Moscow pastel.

7. See, for example, Patricia Simons, "Women in Frames: The Gaze, the Eye, the Profile in Renaissance Portraiture," in *The Expanding Discourse: Feminism and Art History*, eds. Norma Broude and Mary D. Garrard (New York: Icon Editions, 1992), pp. 39–57.

8. The sitter for this work is Mary Dickinson Scott Newbold, whose family commissioned the painting *Portrait of Mrs. Clement B. Newbold* (private collection), in 1895. Mrs. Newbold purchased an important Cassatt pastel, *Young Thomas and His Mother*, which she donated to the Pennsylvania Academy of the Fine Arts, Philadelphia, in 1904.

9. On the changing reputation of the *Small Cowper Madonna*, see David Alan Brown, *Raphael and America* (Washington, D.C.: National Gallery of Art, 1983), pp. 82–6.

10. *Sfumato*, a painting technique that is believed to have originated with Leonardo da Vinci, involves the blending of tones so that forms are defined without clear outlines.

11. In the pastel *Reine Lefebvre and Margot* (Armand Hammer Collection, UCLA), a highly finished version of this same composition, it is more evident that the child is leaning upon the woman's knee.

12. For a discussion of pets in France in this period, and the association of small dogs with girls and women in particular, see Kathleen Kete, *The Beast in the Boudoir: Petkeeping in Nineteenth-Century Paris* (Berkeley, Los Angeles, London: University of California Press, 1994).

13. On Cassatt's "Modern Madonnas," see Nancy Mowll Mathews, "Mary Cassatt and the 'Modern Madonna' of the Nineteenth Century" (unpublished doctoral diss., New York University, 1980), and Ivinski, *Mary Cassatt, the Maternal Body, and Modern Connoisseurship*.

14. Catalogue numbers 28 and 29 were made from the same unrecorded pastel.

Notes on the use of the Catalogue

The discovery of this collection provides us with important new information about the pastel counterproofs of Mary Cassatt. In Adelyn Dohme Breeskin's *Mary Cassatt: A Catalogue Raisonné of the Oils, Pastels, Watercolors, and Drawings* (Washington, D.C.: Smithsonian Institution Press, 1970), only thirteen counterproofs were recorded. In the ensuing years, and with the emergence of this collection, more than 100 additional counterproofs have come to light. This catalogue includes less than half of these works, and a more complete record of Cassatt's counterproof production must await the publication of the forthcoming revised catalogue raisonné, currently being prepared by the Mary Cassatt Catalogue Raisonné Committee.

In the years since the counterproofs were produced, changes have been made to many of the pastels from which they were taken. In some cases, Cassatt herself may have been responsible; in other cases, the pastels have been completely reworked, to the extent that they can no longer be confidently ascribed to the hand of Cassatt. We have sought in this catalogue to associate counterproofs with the pastels from which they were taken, even if changes have since been made to those pastels. If the pastel is illustrated in the Breeskin catalogue raisonné, the Breeskin catalogue number is cited in our catalogue entry following the abbreviation BrCR. Some counterproofs are identified as having been made from pastels that became known only after the publication of the Breeskin catalogue raisonné. This is indicated in our catalogue entry with the words "Pastel counterproof of a work not in Breeskin." (The citation of pastels from which counterproofs were made does not imply that these pastels have been examined by the Mary Cassatt Catalogue Raisonné Committee, nor that decisions regarding their inclusion in the forthcoming catalogue raisonné have yet been made.) In addition, the pastels from which seven of the counterproof images in this catalogue were made remain unpublished and unlocated; this is indicated in our catalogue with the phrase "Pastel counterproof of an unrecorded pastel."

Based on our knowledge of Vollard's developing relationship with Cassatt in the early 1900s and on the date of the latest pastel for which we have a counterproof (*Child Leaning Against Her Young Mother*, ca. 1913 [5]), we believe that the counterproofs were made over a period of time, possibly between 1905 and 1915. In the case of *Head of Margot Looking to Right* [45], we know that this counterproof must have been made before late 1908, because the pastel from which it was taken (now in the Indianapolis Museum of Art) was purchased from Vollard and shipped to the United States by December 1908.

Titles

For the counterproofs that were made from pastels published in the Breeskin catalogue raisonné, we have used the Breeskin titles in our catalogue entries. For works that have never before been published, we have assigned titles. All titles are subject to revision in the forthcoming catalogue raisonné.

Dates

The first dates listed in our catalogue entries are those assigned by Breeskin to the pastels from which the counterproofs were made. More recent research by the Mary Cassatt Catalogue Raisonné Committee is leading us to redate many of these works. Though this redating is subject to change upon the publication of the revised catalogue raisonné, we have indicated possible new dates in brackets. In the case of counterproofs made from pastels that were discovered after the publication of the Breeskin catalogue and counterproofs made from unrecorded pastels, proposed dates are given in brackets.

Signatures and inscriptions

If a counterproof includes a reverse signature transferred from the original pastel, this is noted in our catalogue entry by the term "counterproof signature." If the work is signed or inscribed in any other manner than "Mary Cassatt," this is indicated in the catalogue entry.

Dimensions

All of the counterproofs (with the exception of *Smiling Sara in a Big Hat Holding Her Dog (No. 1)* [12]) are on tissue-thin Japan paper, mounted on wove paper. The dimensions given are those of the image or mat opening, height before width in both inches and centimeters.

1.

Mother Combing Sara's Hair (No. 2)

Pastel counterproof of BrCR 348
ca. 1901 [ca. 1901–1902]
on Japan paper
with counterproof signature
18¼ × 23⅞ in. (46.3 × 60.8 cm)

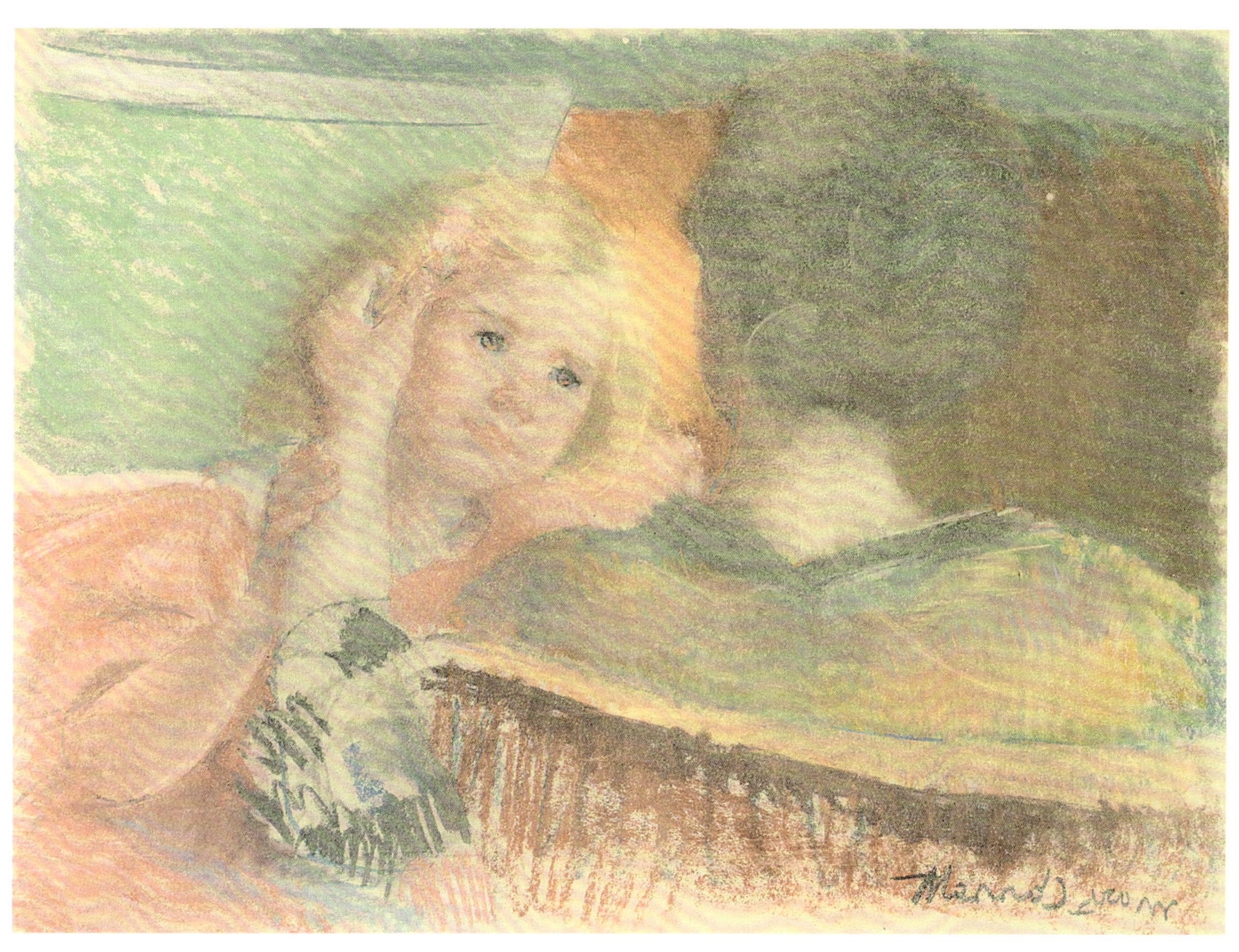

2.

The Banjo Lesson

Pastel counterproof of BrCR 238
1894 [ca. 1893]
on Japan paper
with counterproof signature
28¼ × 23 in. (72 × 58.3 cm)

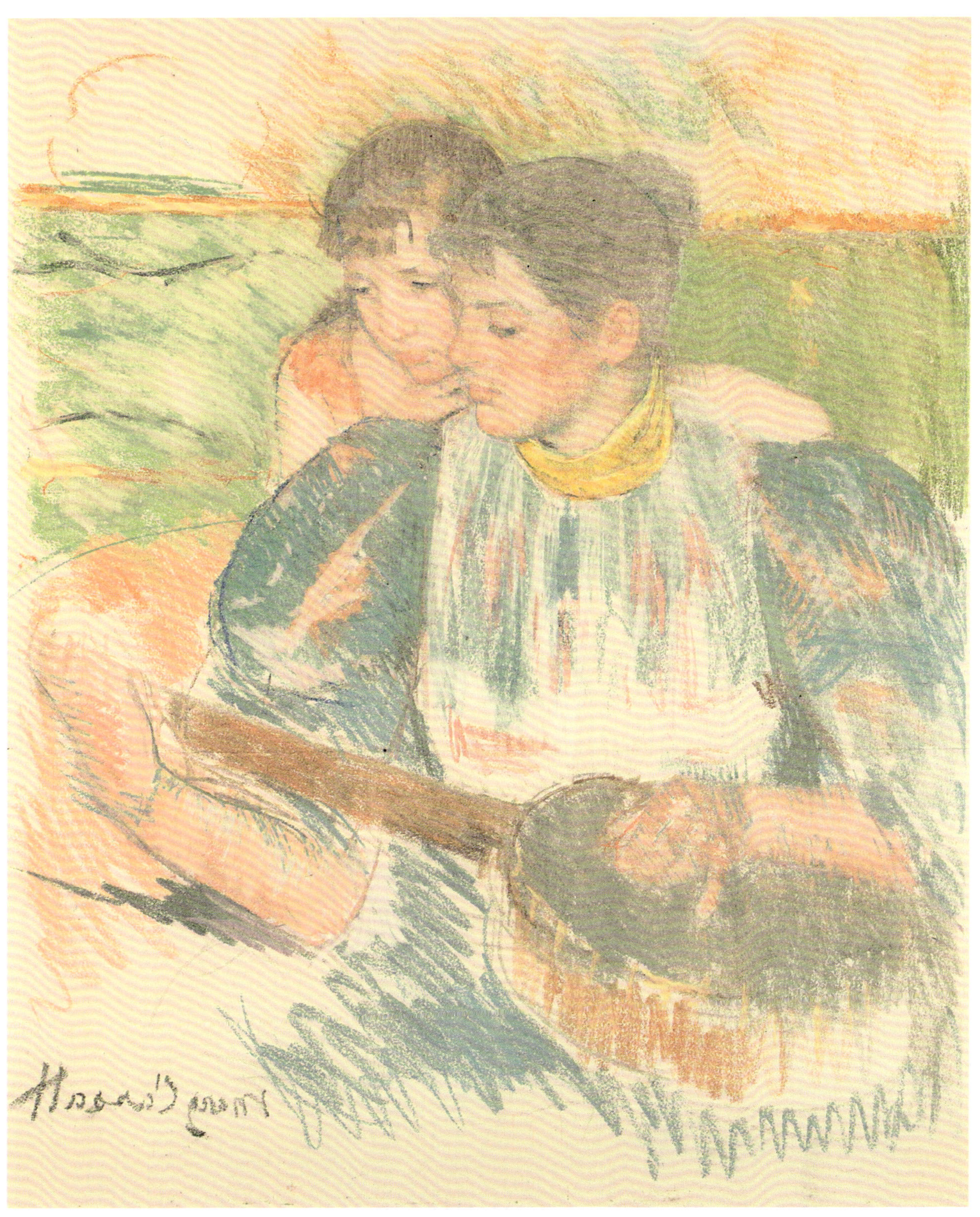

3.

A Kiss for Baby Anne (No. 1)

Pastel counterproof of BrCR 264
ca. 1897 [ca. 1897–1898]
on Japan paper
24¾ × 20½ in. (63 × 52 cm)

The pastel, BrCR 264, appears to
have been signed after this counterproof
was made.

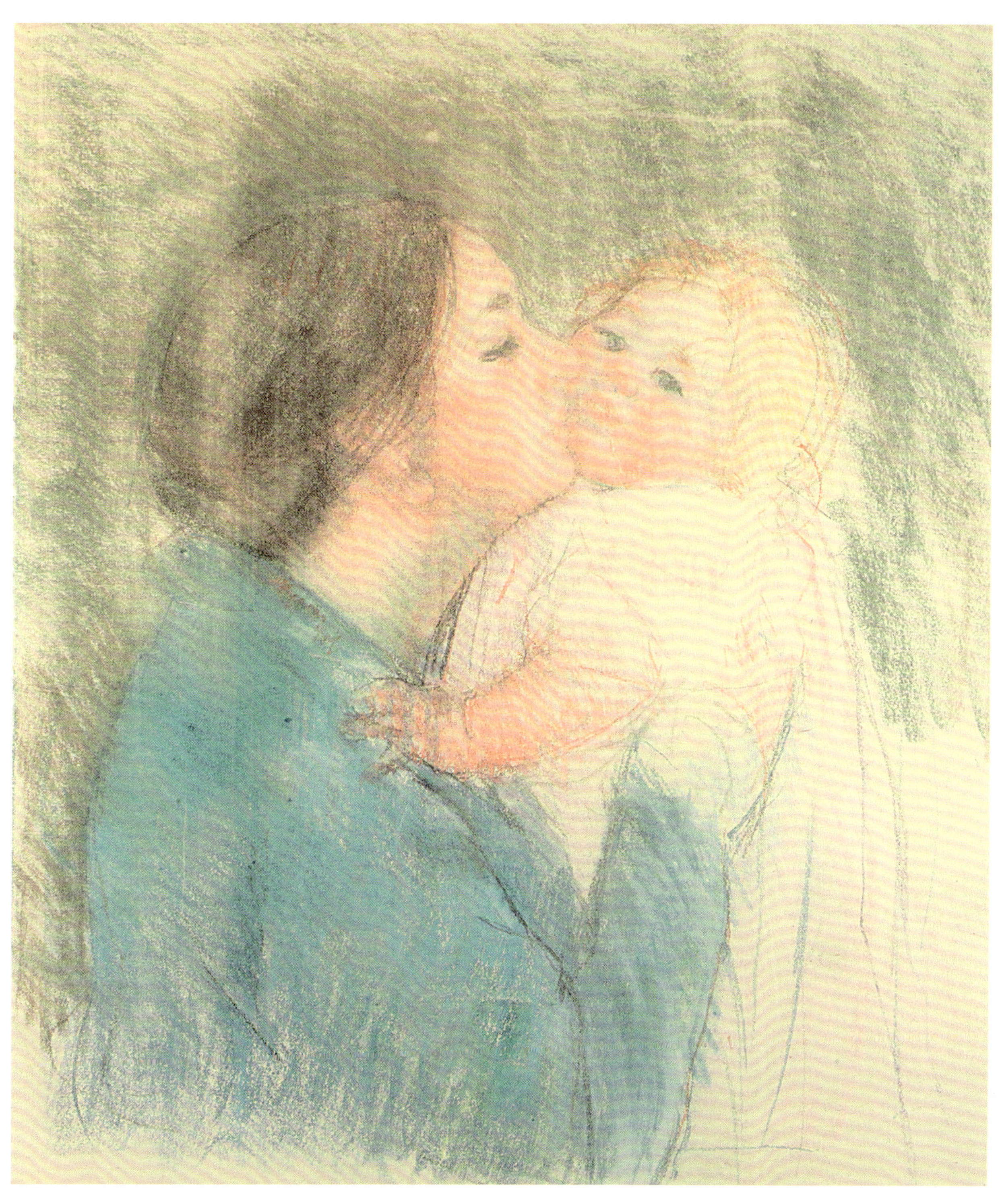

4.

Portrait of a Young Woman in Green

Pastel counterproof of BrCR 290
ca. 1898 [ca. 1895]
on Japan paper
with counterproof signatures: Mary Ca[…]/M. Cassatt
24⅝ × 18¾ in. (62.5 × 47.7 cm)

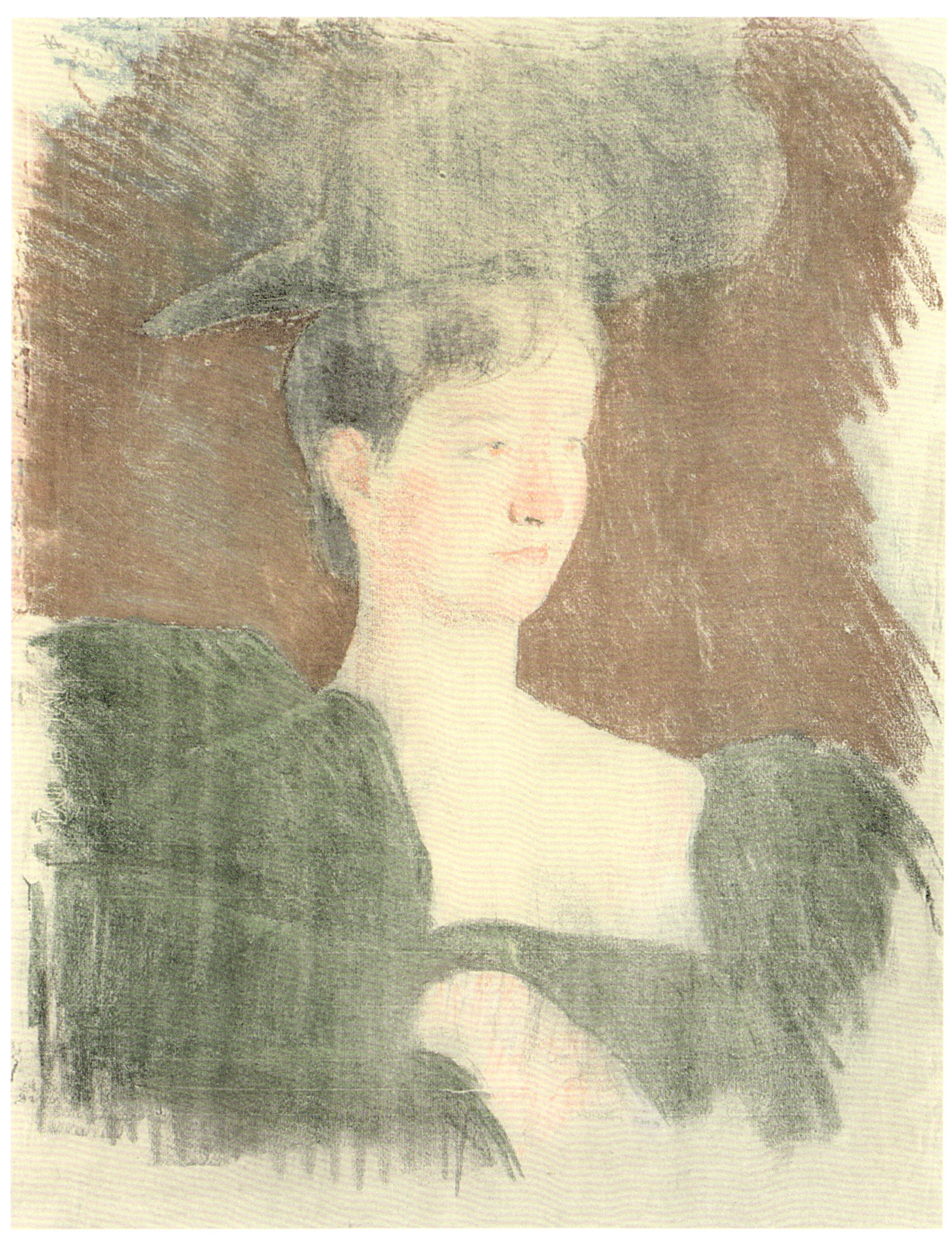

5.

Child Leaning Against Her Young Mother

Pastel counterproof of BrCR 592
ca. 1913
on Japan paper
with counterproof signature
25½ × 19 in. (64.8 × 48.3 cm)

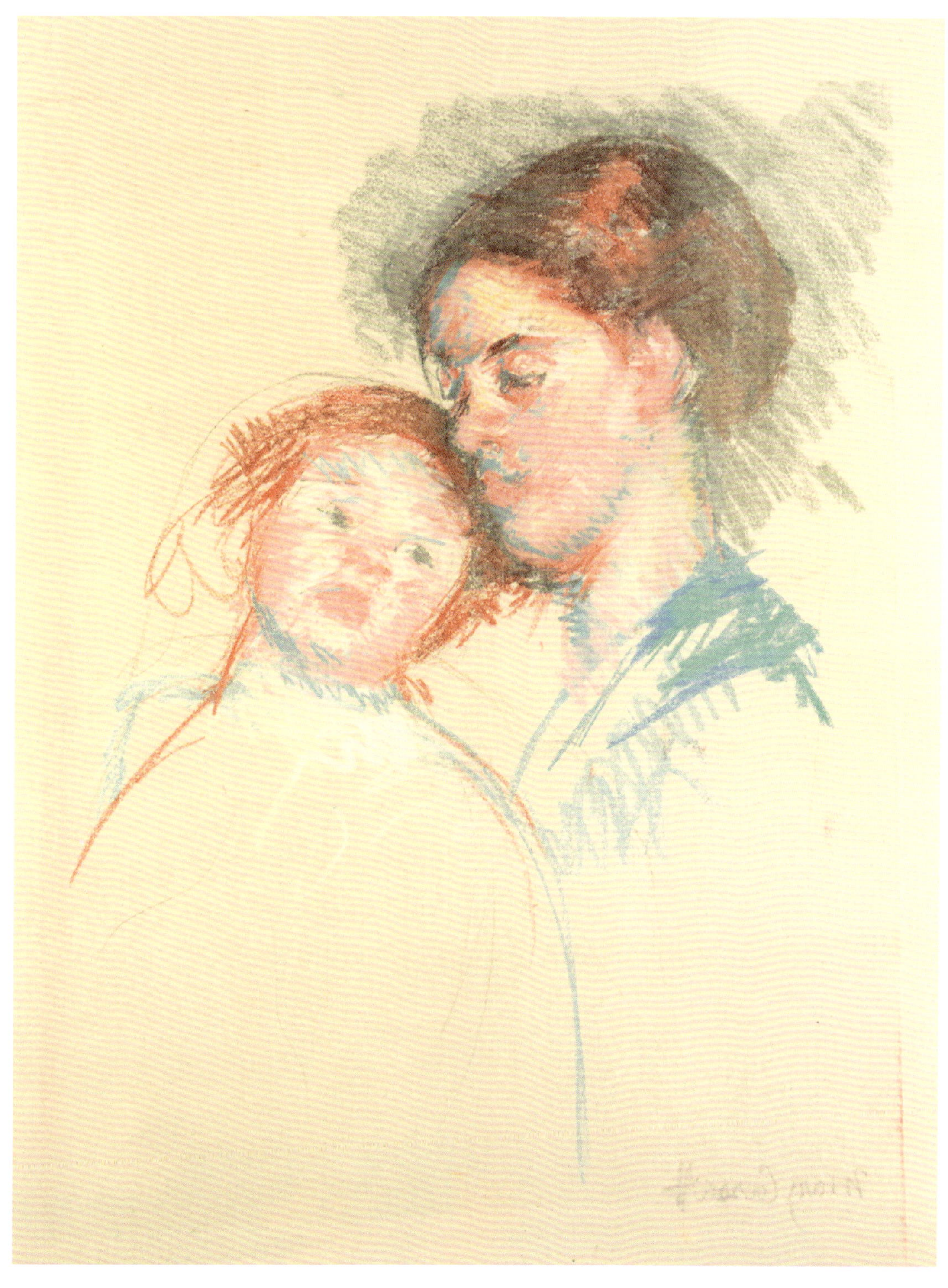

6.

Margot Wearing a Blue Gauze Bonnet

Pastel counterproof of a work not in Breeskin
[ca. 1900–1901]
on Japan paper
with counterproof signature
19⅛ × 17¾ in. (48.6 × 45 cm)

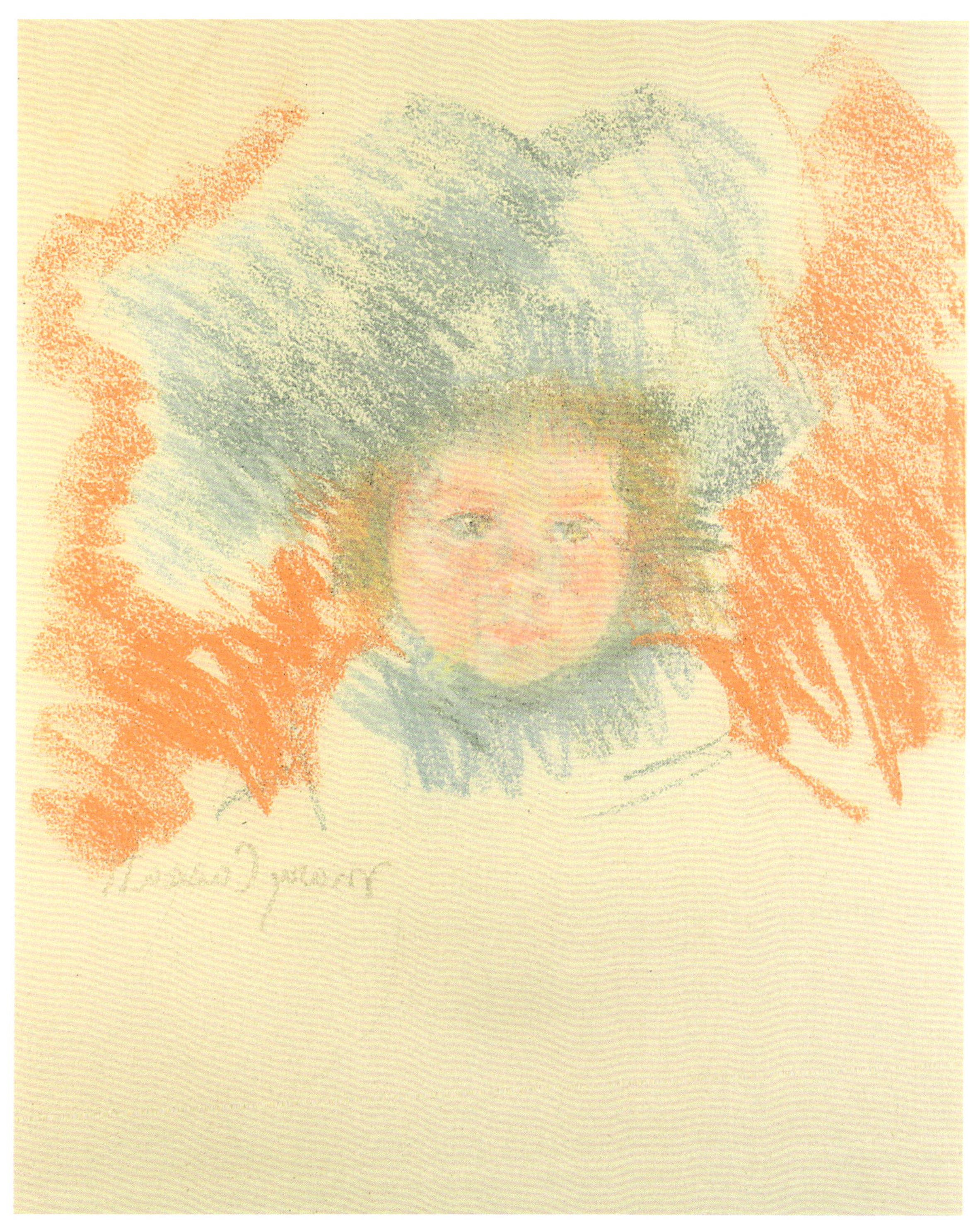

7.

**Margot in a Dark Red Costume Seated
on a Round-Backed Chair**

Pastel counterproof of BrCR 426
ca. 1902 [ca. 1899]
on Japan paper
with counterproof signature
24¾ × 20⅞ in. (63 × 53 cm)

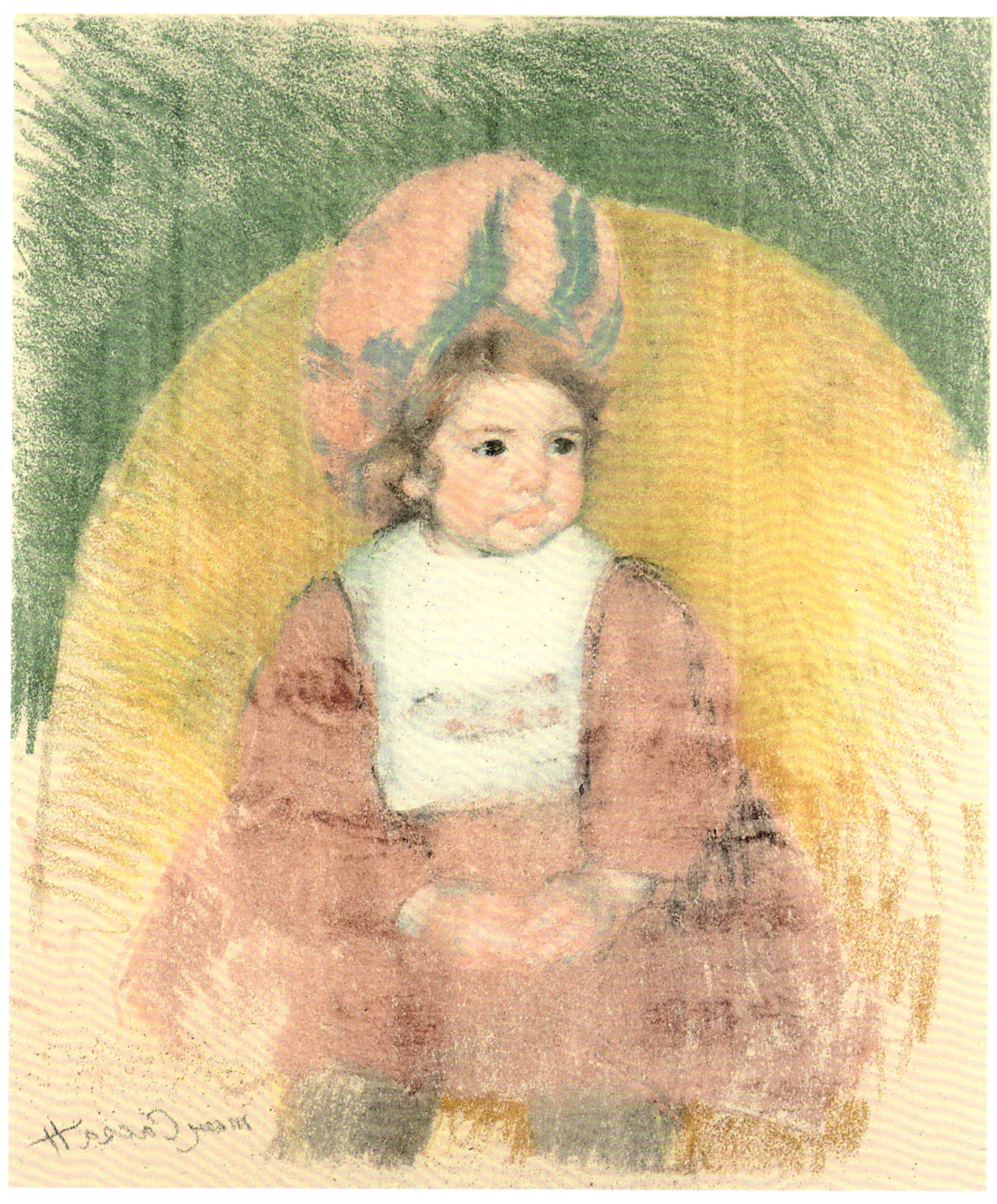

8.

Madame and Her Maid

Pastel counterproof of BrCR 241
ca. 1894 [ca. 1894–1895]
on Japan paper
with counterproof signature
19⅞ × 28½ in. (50.5 × 72.5 cm)

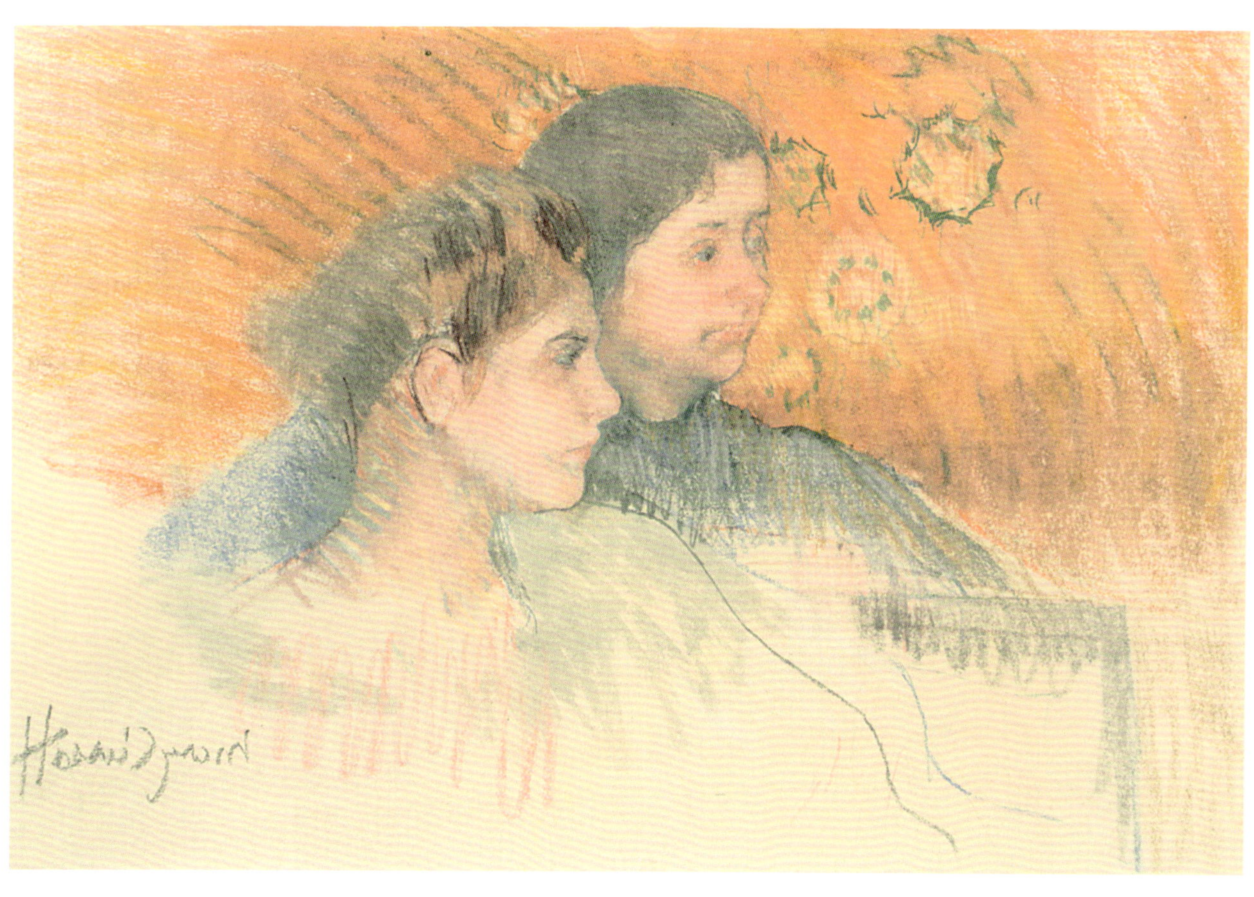

9.

Simone Seated on the Grass
Next to Her Mother

Pastel counterproof of BrCR 453
ca. 1904 [ca. 1902]
on Japan paper
with counterproof signature
27⅞ × 23 in. (70.8 × 58.5 cm)

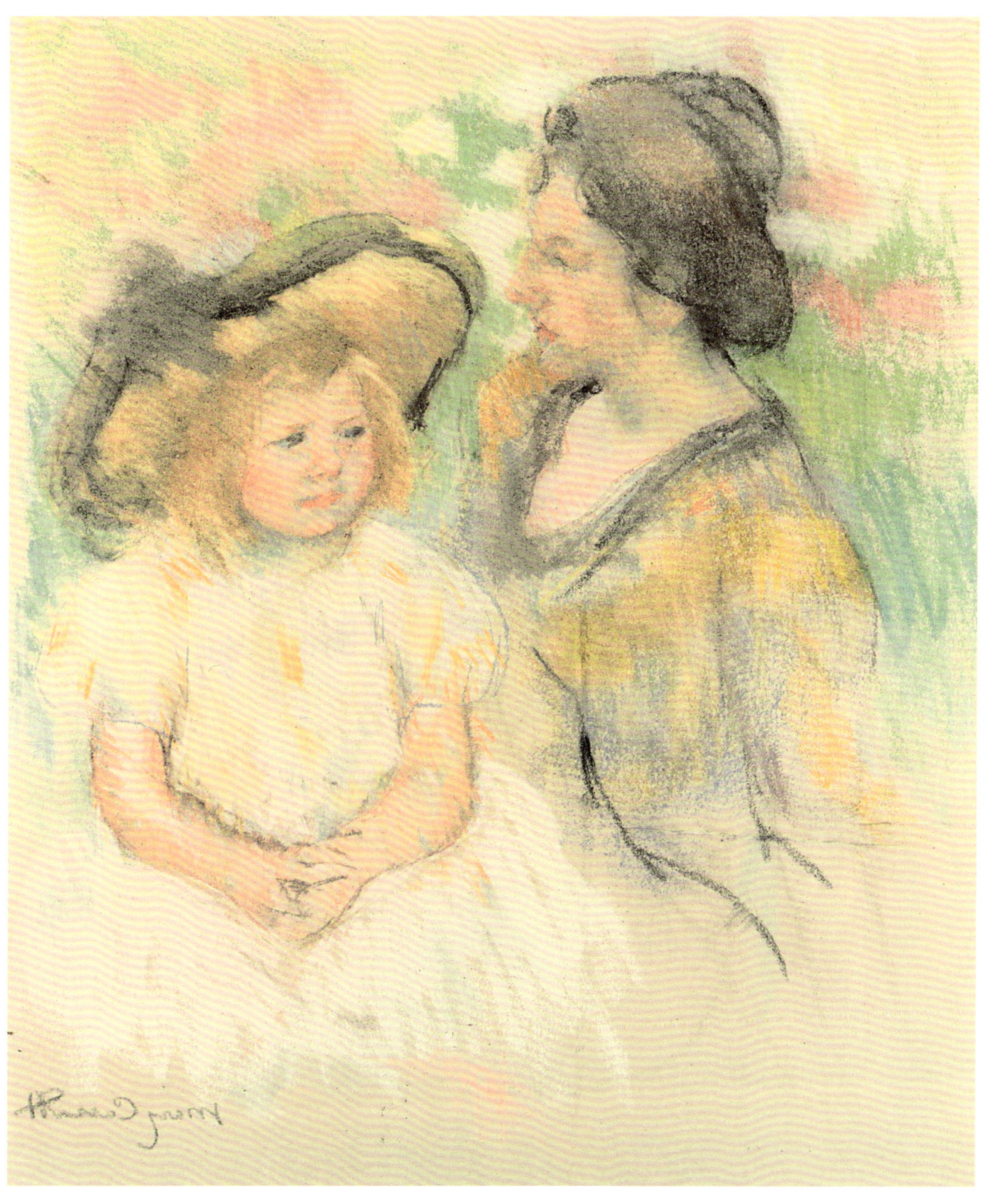

10.

Simone in a Round-Backed Upholstered Chair

Pastel counterproof of BrCR 435
ca. 1903 [ca. 1900–1901]
on Japan paper
with counterproof signature
18⅞ × 18⅛ in. (48 × 46 cm)

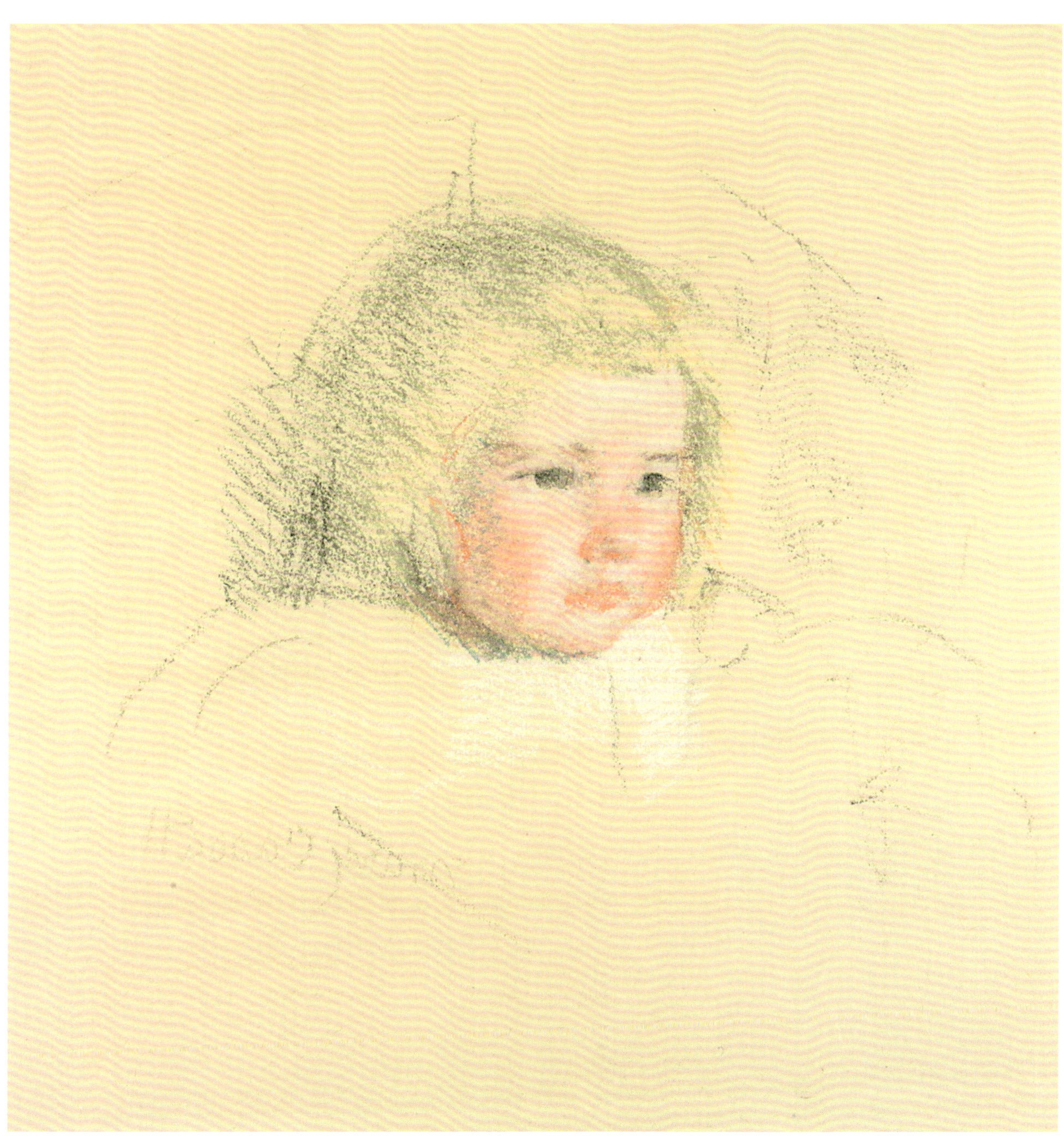

11.

Sketch of a Mother Looking
Down at Thomas

Pastel counterproof of BrCR 224
ca. 1893 [ca. 1894–1895]
on Japan paper
with counterproof signature
20⅛ × 23 in. (51 × 58.5 cm)

The image in this counterproof has been
cropped to a horizontal format, omitting the
lightly sketched lower part of the composition
seen in the pastel, BrCR 224.

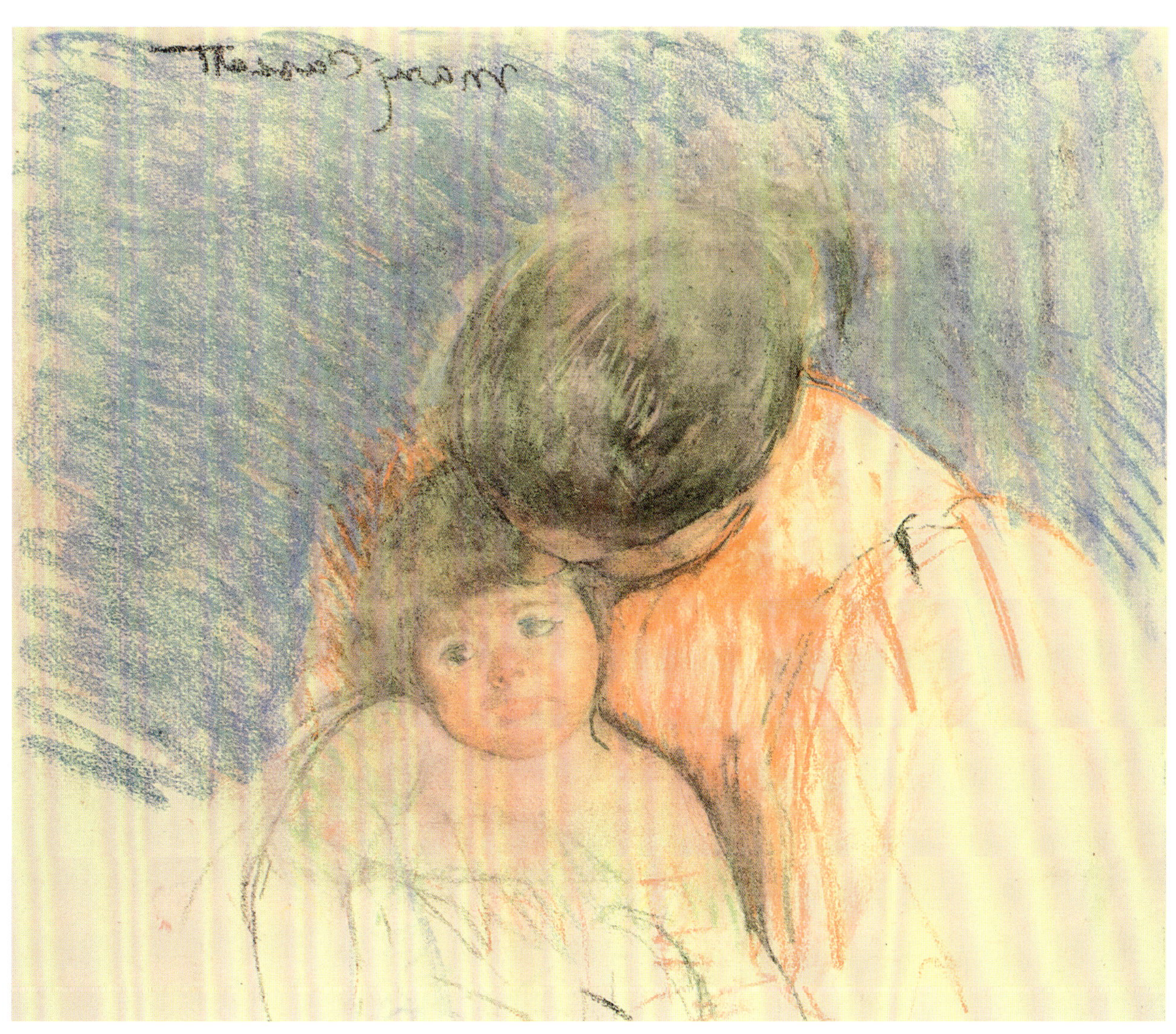

12.

Smiling Sara in a Big Hat Holding Her Dog (No. 1)

Pastel counterproof of BrCR 373
ca. 1901 [ca. 1901–1903]
on wove paper, mounted on board
21¾ × 16½ in. (55.5 × 42 cm)

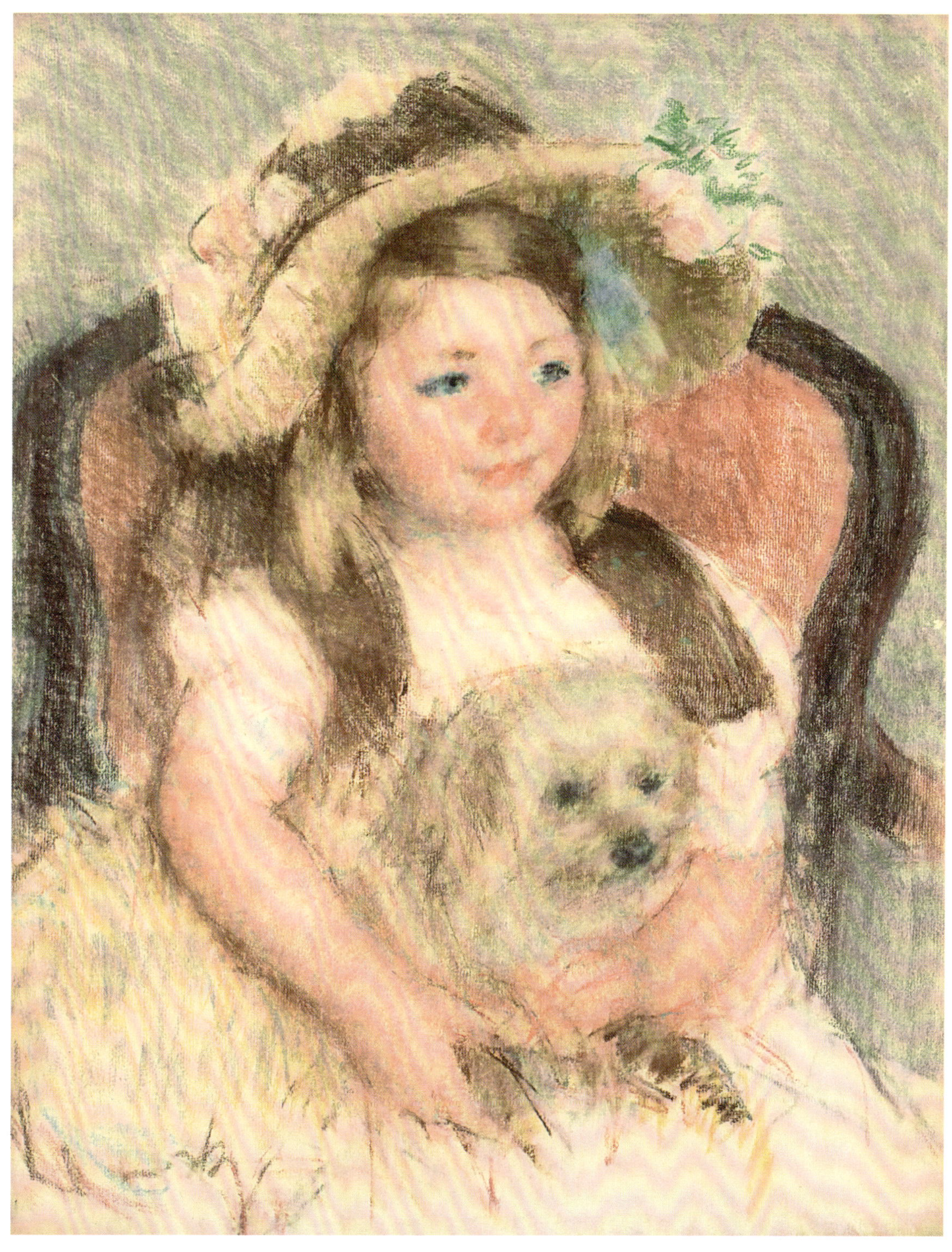

13.

Sara in a Large Flowered Hat, Looking Right, Holding Her Dog

Pastel counterproof of BrCR 377
ca. 1901 [ca. 1901–1903]
on Japan paper
with counterproof signature
26¼ × 22 in. (66.5 × 55.8 cm)

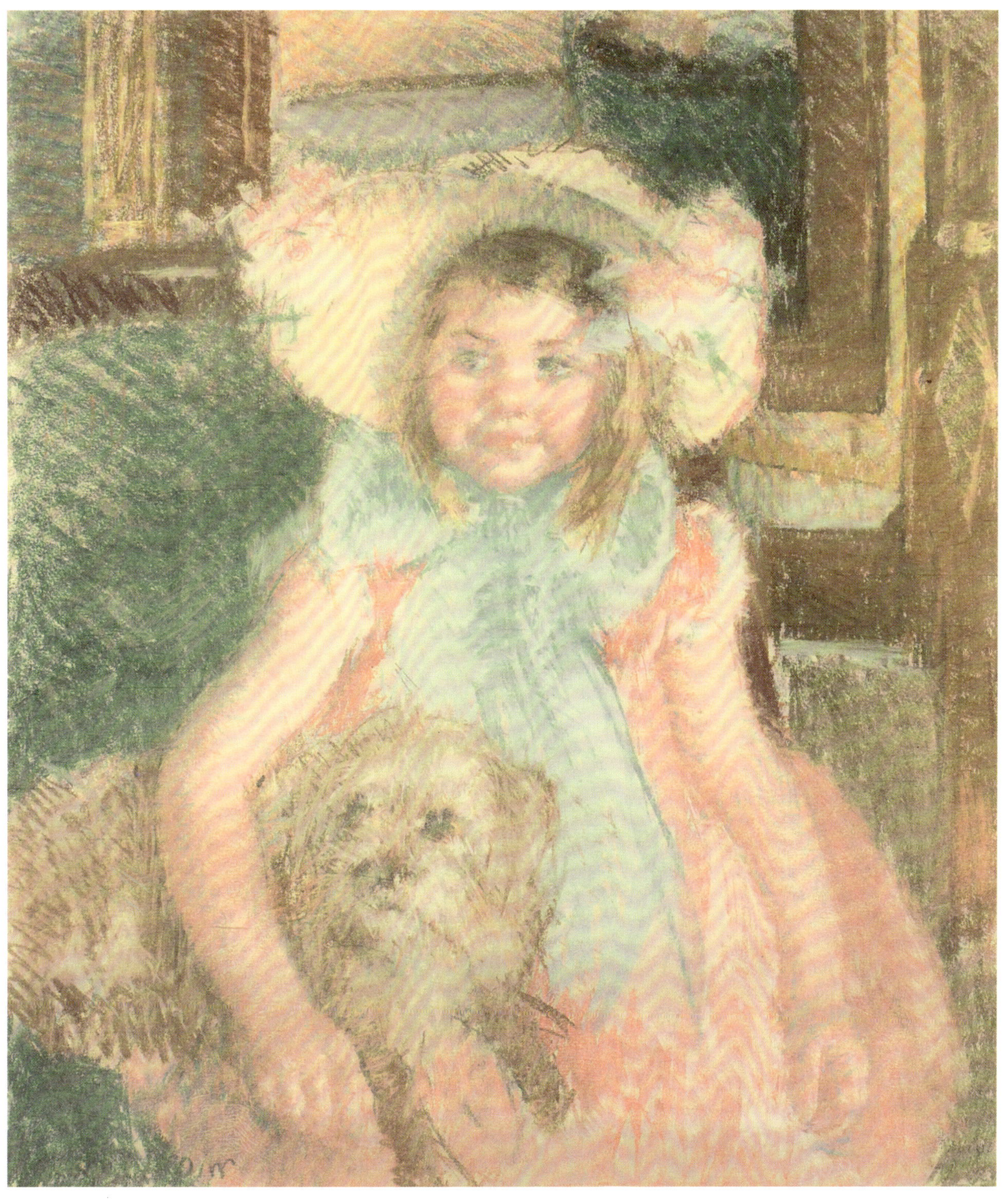

14.

Margot in a Bonnet

Pastel counterproof of an unrecorded pastel
[ca. 1902–1903]
on Japan paper
with counterproof signature
23¼ × 17¾ in. (59 × 45.1 cm)

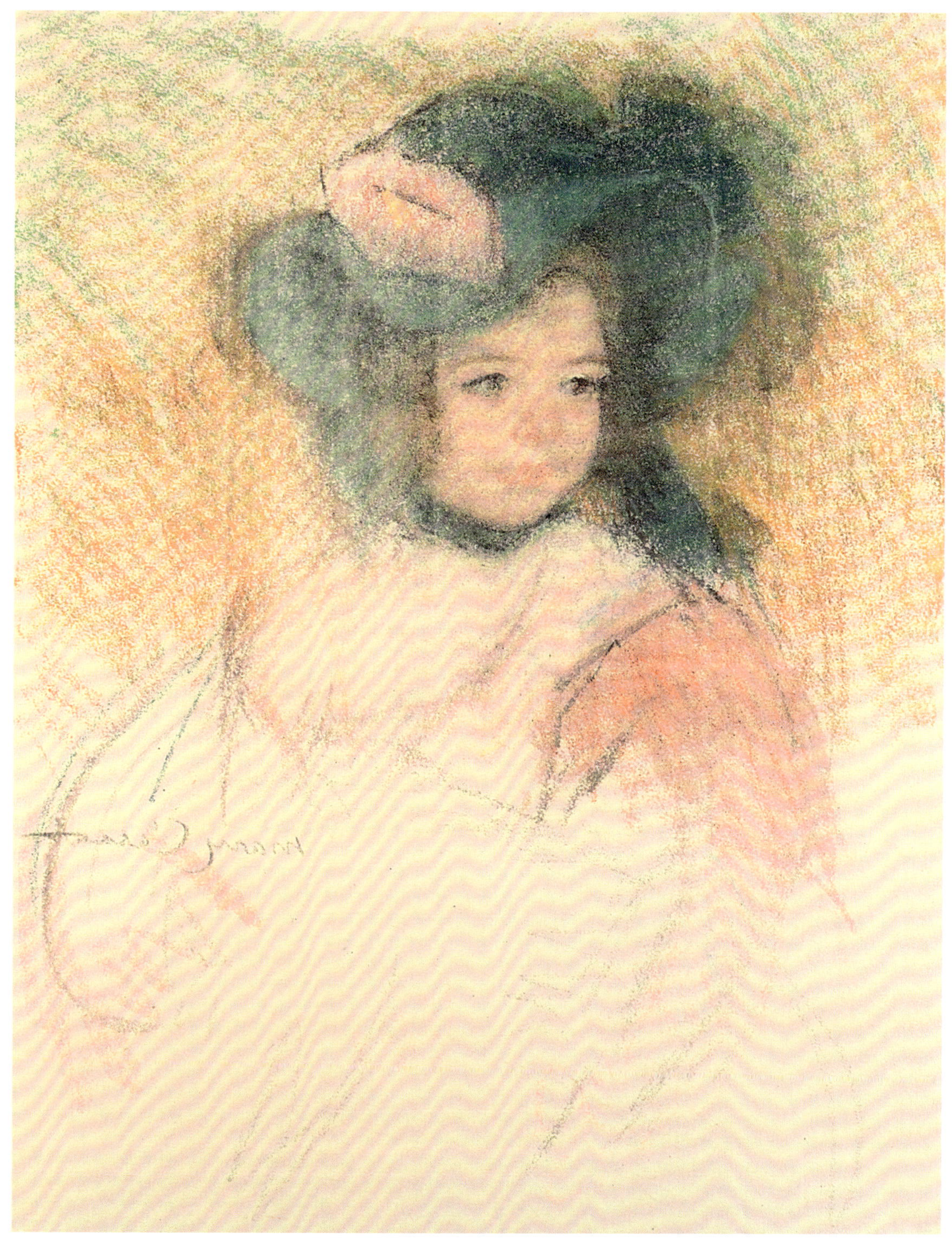

15.

Sara and Her Dog

Pastel counterproof of a work not in Breeskin
[ca. 1901–1903]
on Japan paper
with counterproof signature
22½ × 17 in. (57 × 43.2 cm)

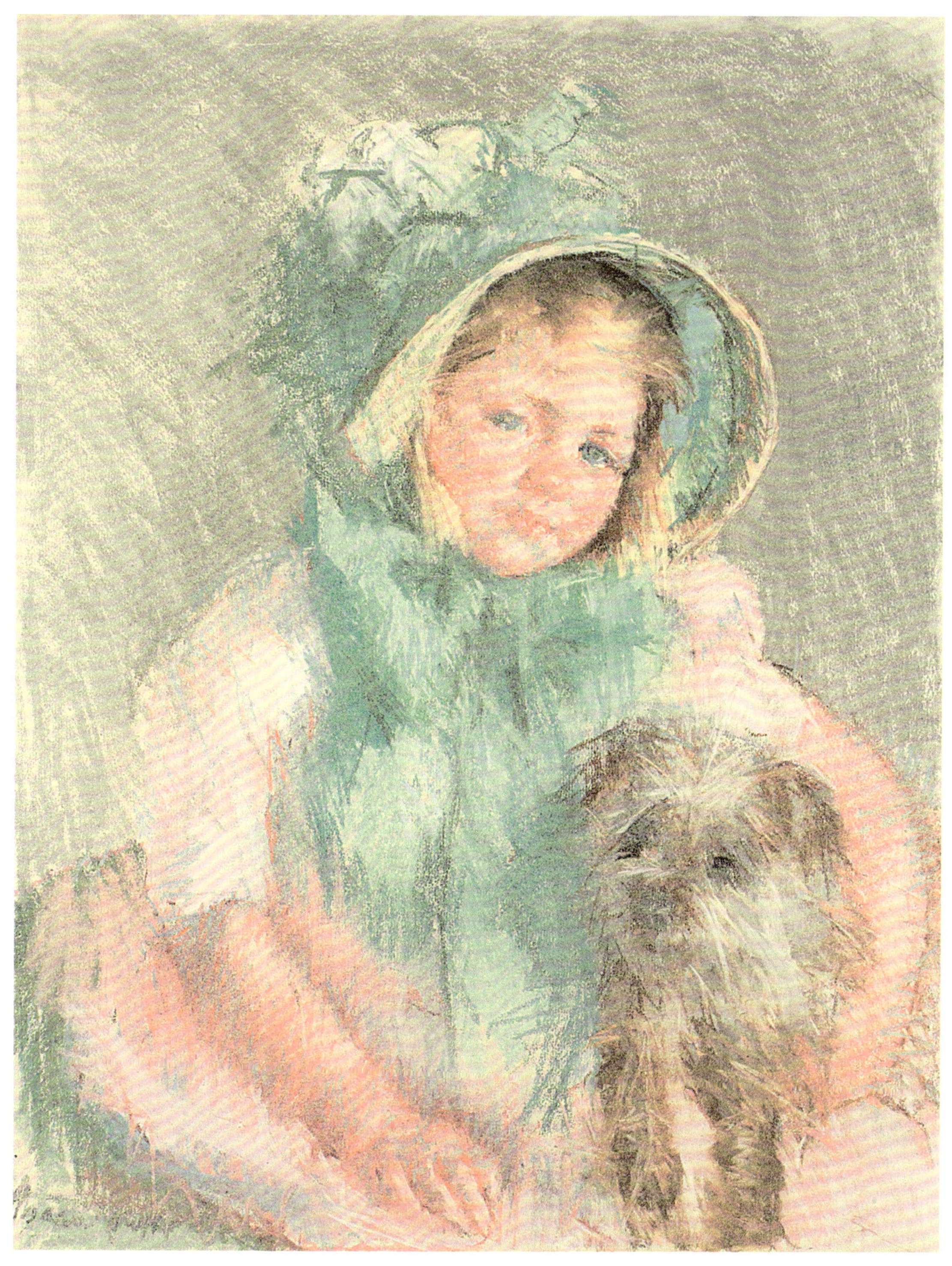

16.

Girl Wearing a Hat with a Blue Bow

Pastel counterproof of an unrecorded pastel
[ca. 1901–1903]
on Japan paper
with counterproof signature
22 × 17½ in. (56 × 44.5 cm)

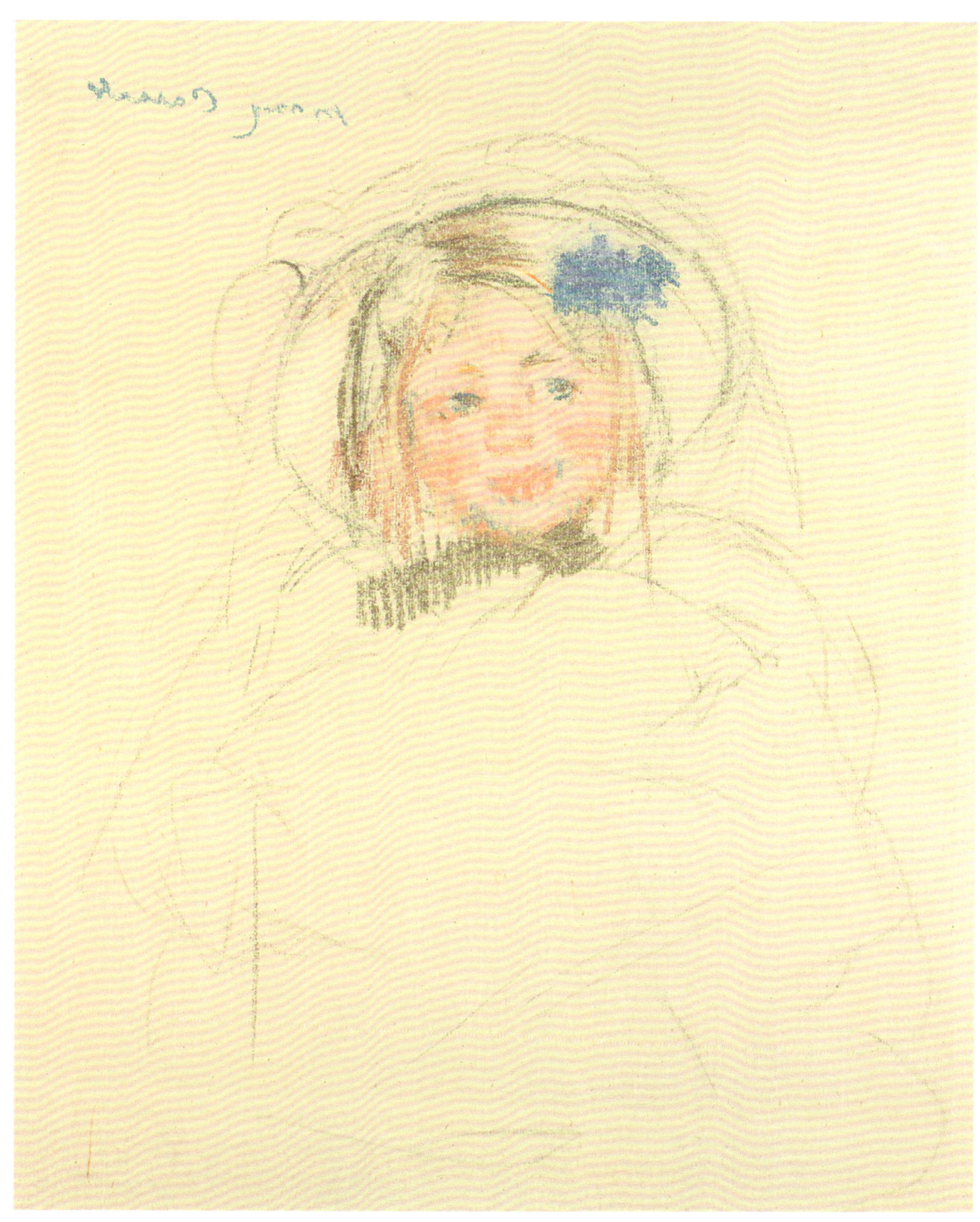

17.

Sara in a Dark Bonnet Holding Her Dog

Pastel counterproof of BrCR 372
ca. 1901 [ca. 1901–1903]
on Japan paper
with indistinct counterproof signature
22⅞ × 17 in. (58.2 × 43.2 cm)

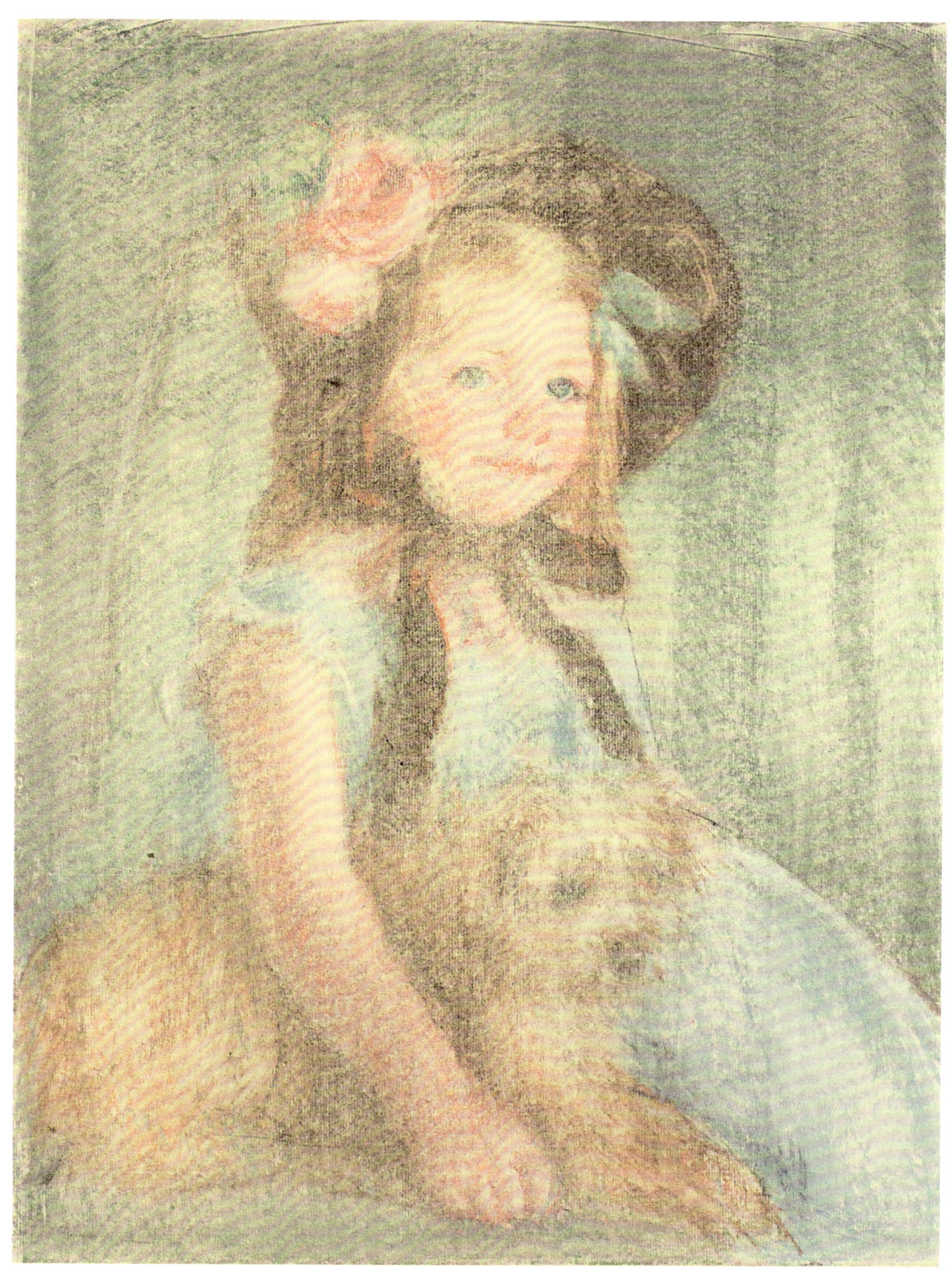

18.

Head of Simone in a Green Bonnet with Wavy Brim (No. 2)

Pastel counterproof of BrCR 458
ca. 1904 [ca. 1901–1903]
on Japan paper
with counterproof signatures upper and lower left
21½ × 17⅝ in. (54.6 × 44.8 cm)

The bonnet in this counterproof appears more
teal than green, as it is described in the Breeskin
title. The pastel, BrCR 458, has been cropped to
an oblong format.

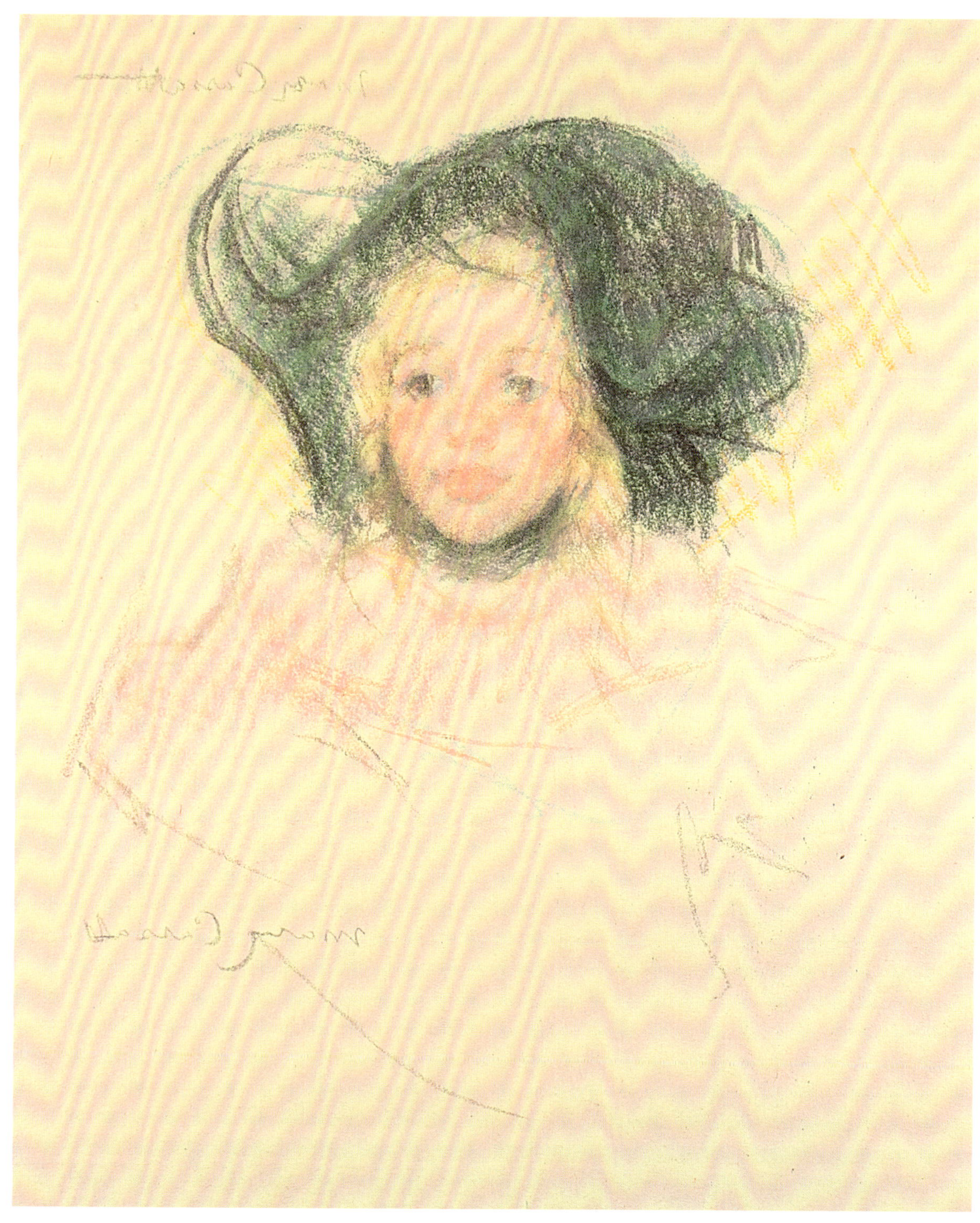

19.

Girl in a Hat with a Black Ribbon

Pastel counterproof of an unrecorded pastel
[ca. 1902]
on Japan paper
with counterproof signature
17¾ × 21⅛ in. (45 × 53.7 cm)

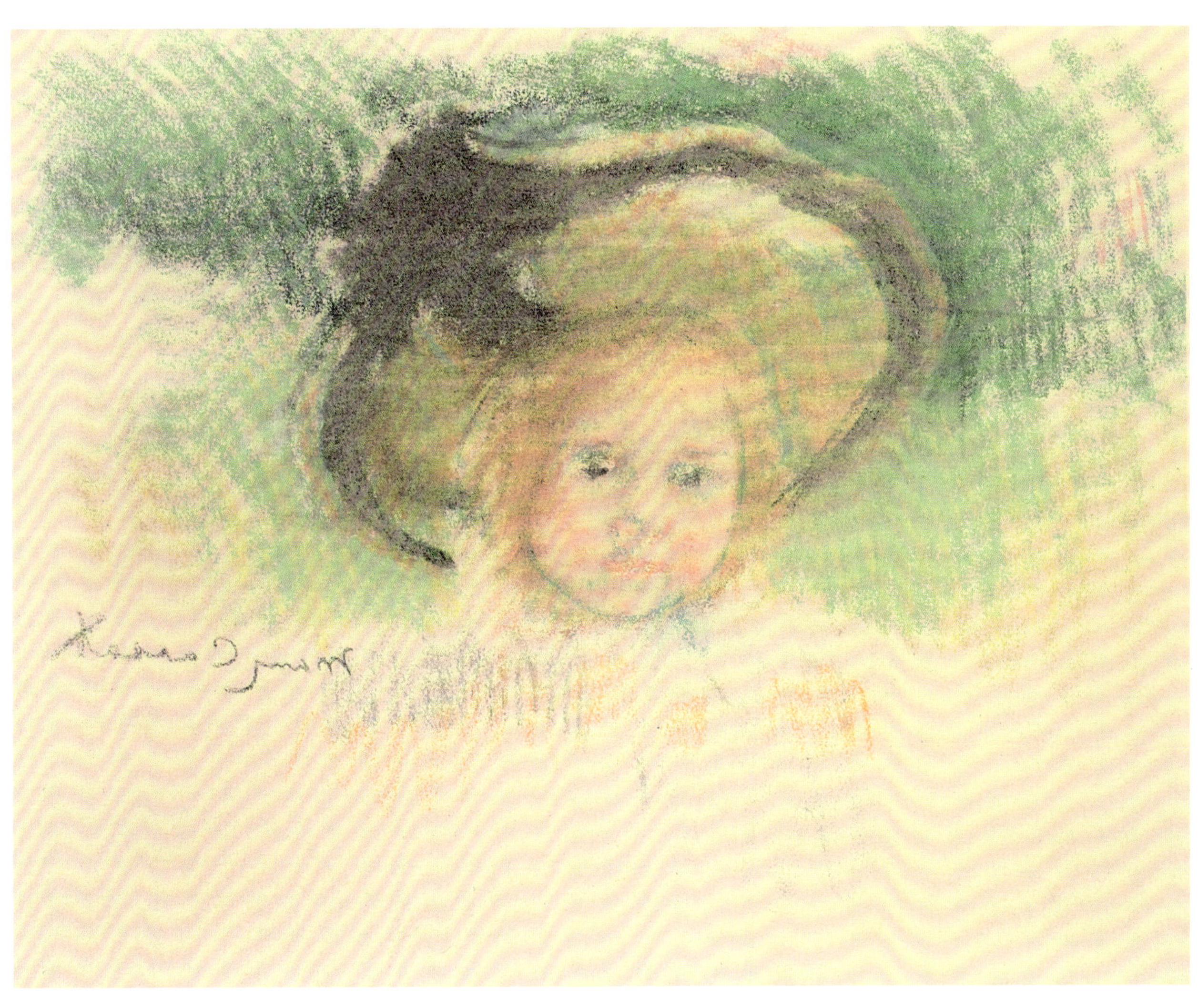

20.

Bust Length Sketch of Margot in a Big Hat and a Red Dress

Pastel counterproof of a work not in Breeskin
[ca. 1902–1903]
on Japan paper
with counterproof signature
23½ × 19 in. (59.7 × 48.3 cm)

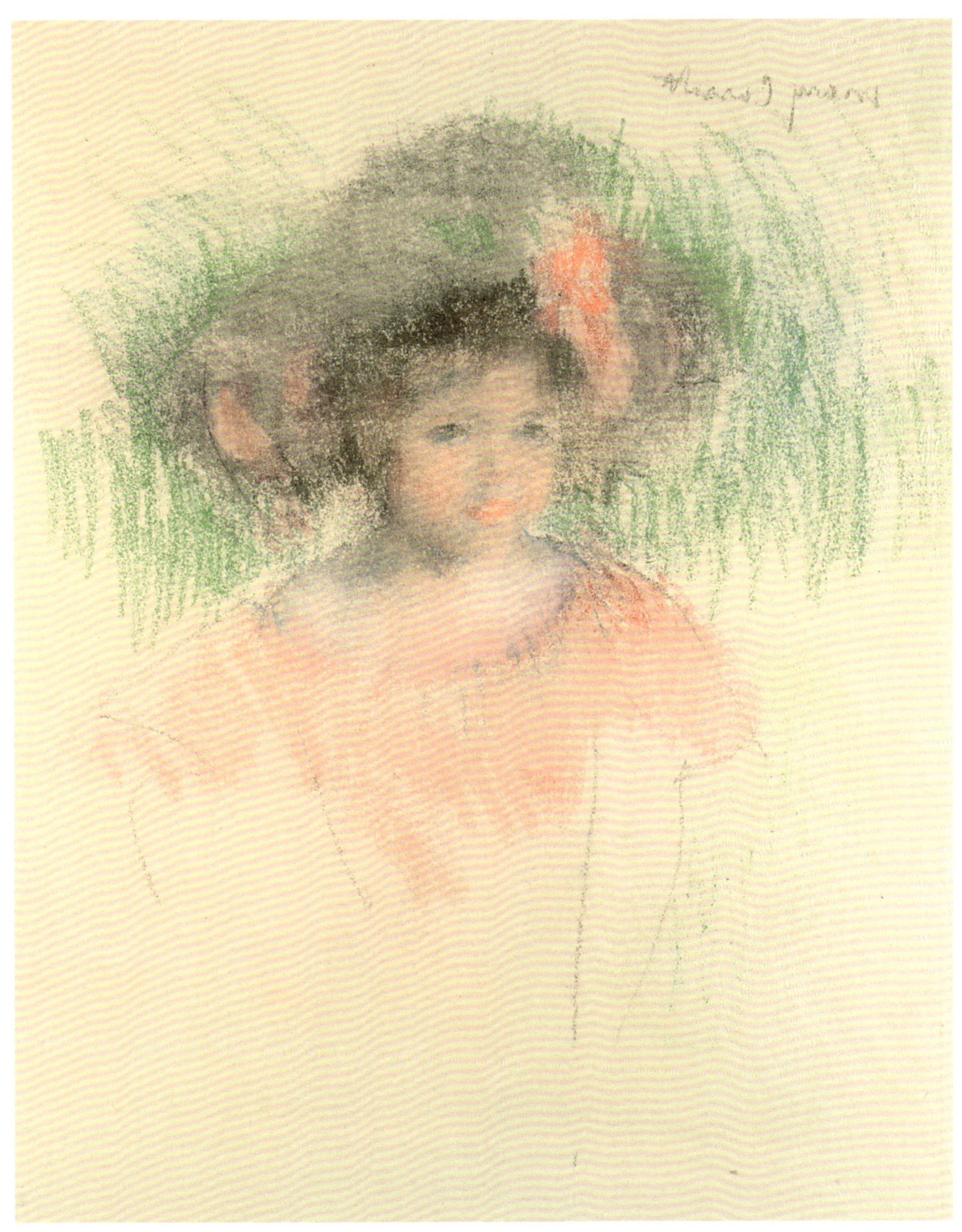

21.

Reine Lefebvre with Blond Baby
and Sara Holding a Cat

Pastel counterproof of BrCR 404
ca. 1902 [ca. 1902–1903]
on Japan paper
with counterproof inscription and signature: à Mons. Vollard/
avec mes compliments […]/Mary Cassatt
31½ × 23¼ in. (80 × 59 cm)

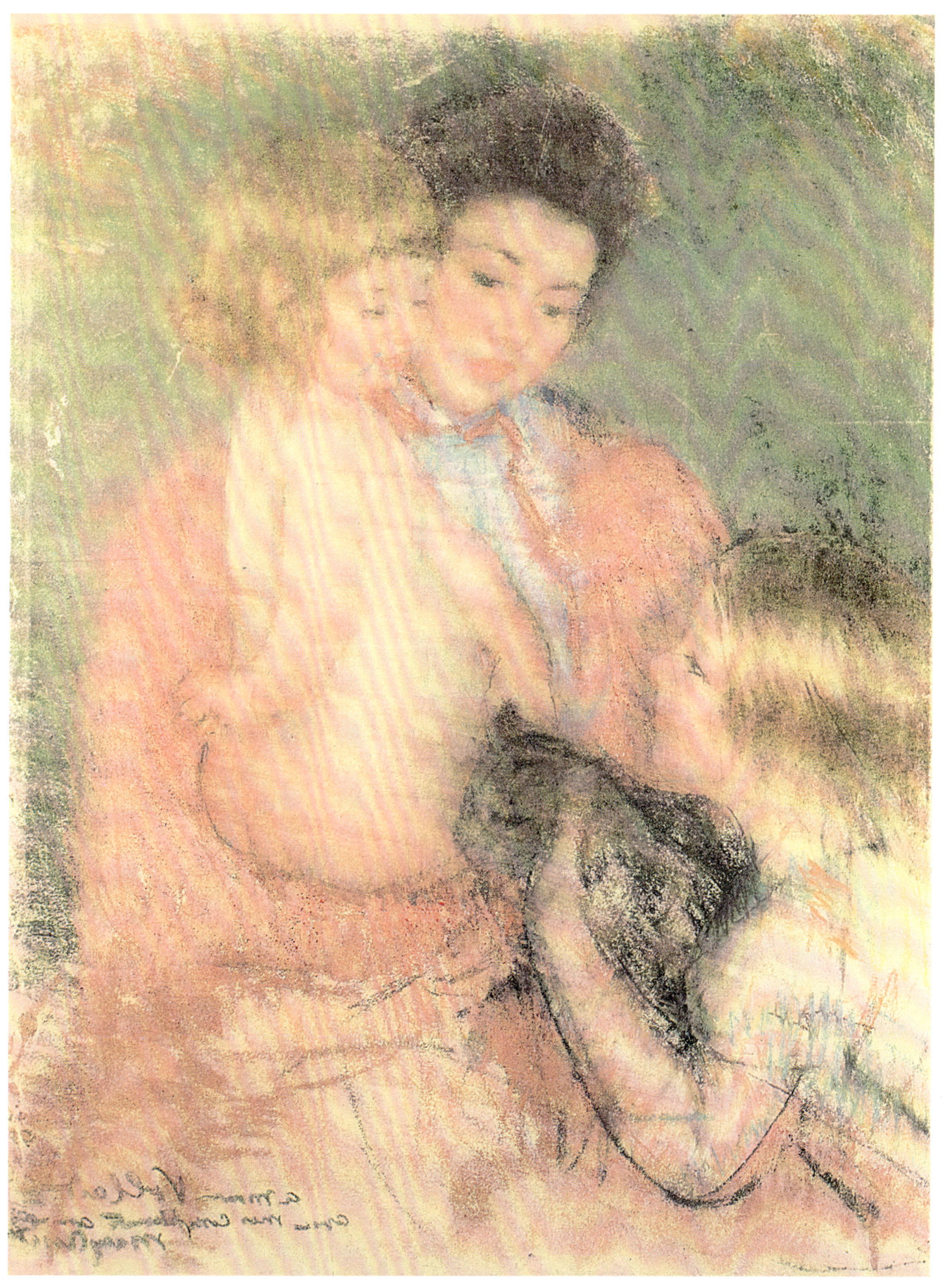

22.

Baby Charles Looking Over
His Mother's Shoulder (No. 2)

Pastel counterproof of BrCR 324
ca. 1900
on Japan paper
with indistinct counterproof signature
and illegible inscription
28 × 23 in. (71.3 × 58.5 cm)

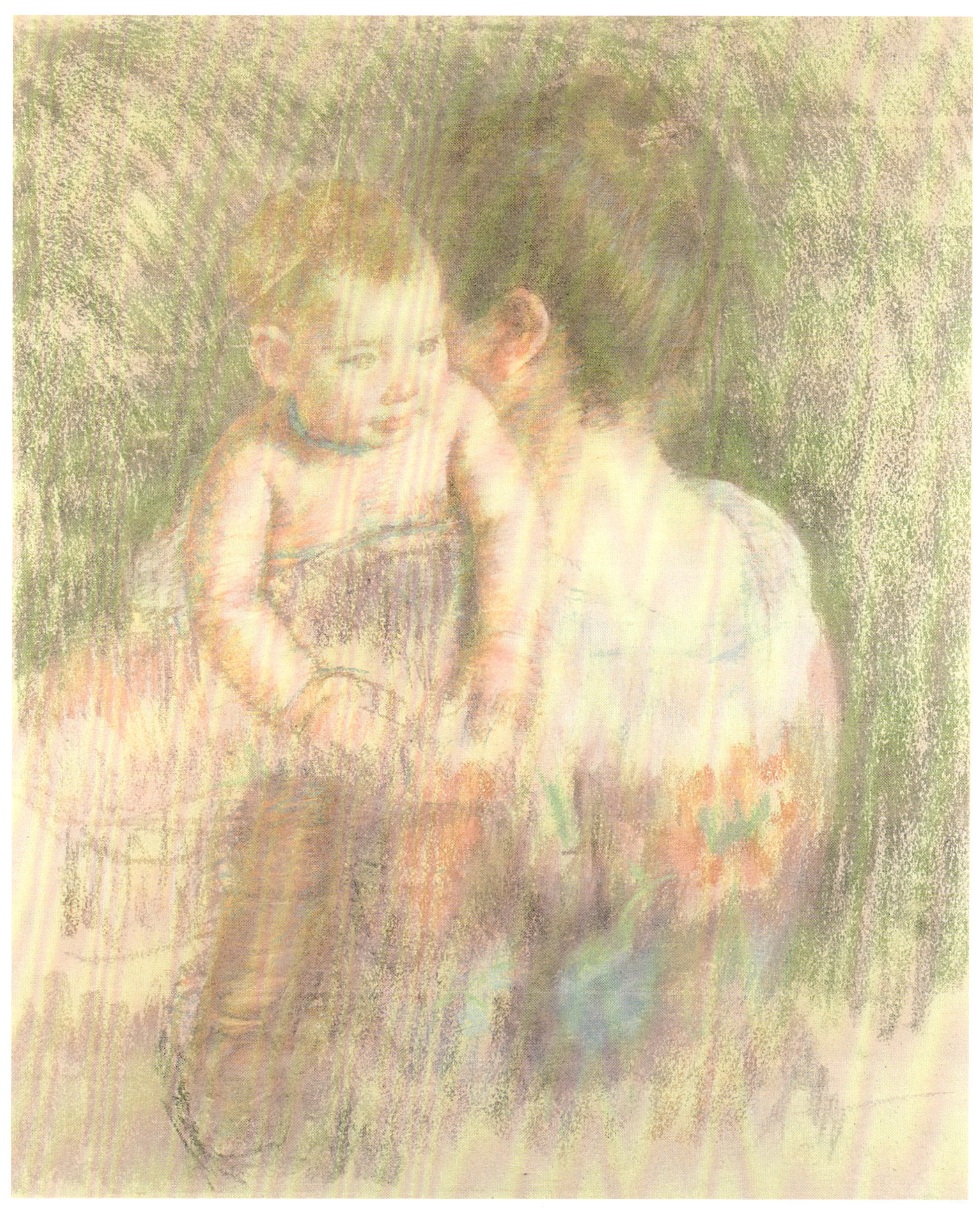

23.

Nicolle and Her Mother

Pastel counterproof of BrCR 326
ca. 1900 [ca. 1898–1899]
on Japan paper
with counterproof signature
30⅝ × 23⅜ in. (77.8 × 59.4 cm)

The original signature, which appears in reverse
on the counterproof, is no longer visible on BrCR 326.
The pastel now bears another signature, evidently
added after this counterproof was taken.

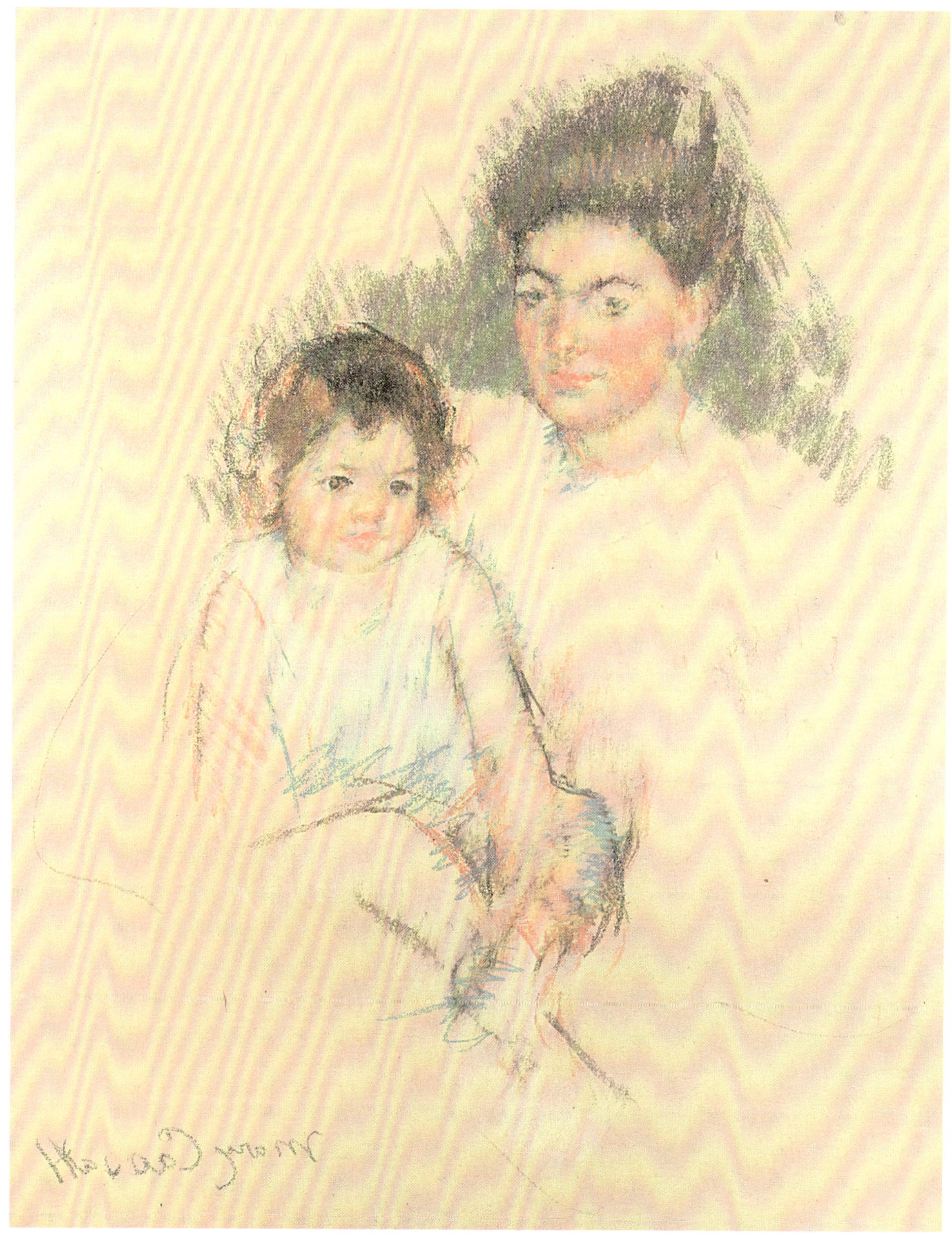

24.

Woman and Child in Front of a Fruit Tree

Pastel counterproof of an unrecorded pastel
[ca. 1893–1894]
on Japan paper
with counterproof signature: M. Cassatt
22¼ × 17¾ in. (56.5 × 45 cm)

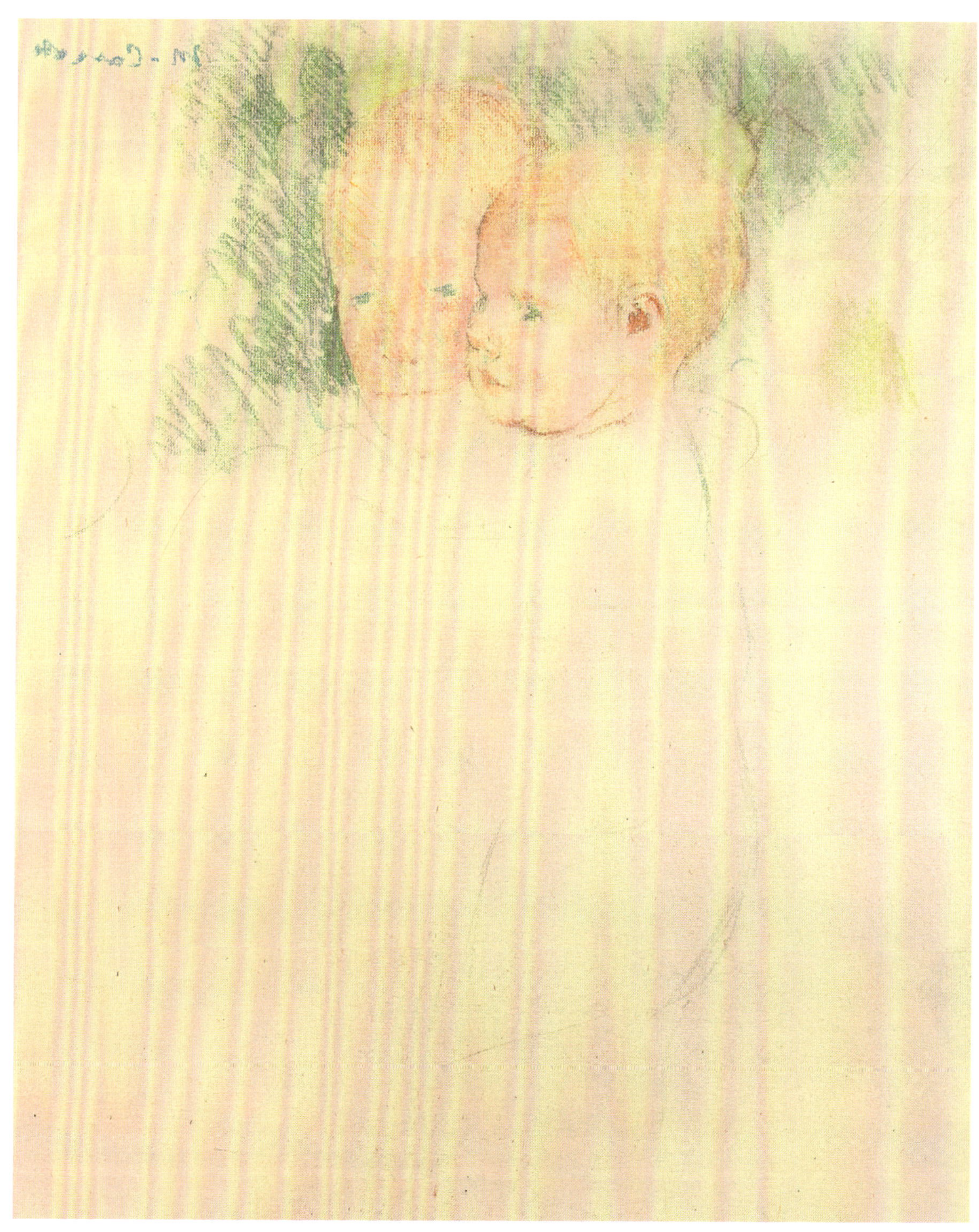

M. Cassatt

25.

Study of Margot in a Fluffy Hat

Pastel counterproof of BrCR 428
ca. 1902 [ca. 1901–1903]
on Japan paper
with counterproof signature
28⅜ × 23¼ in. (72 × 59 cm)

The pastel, BrCR 428, has been cropped.

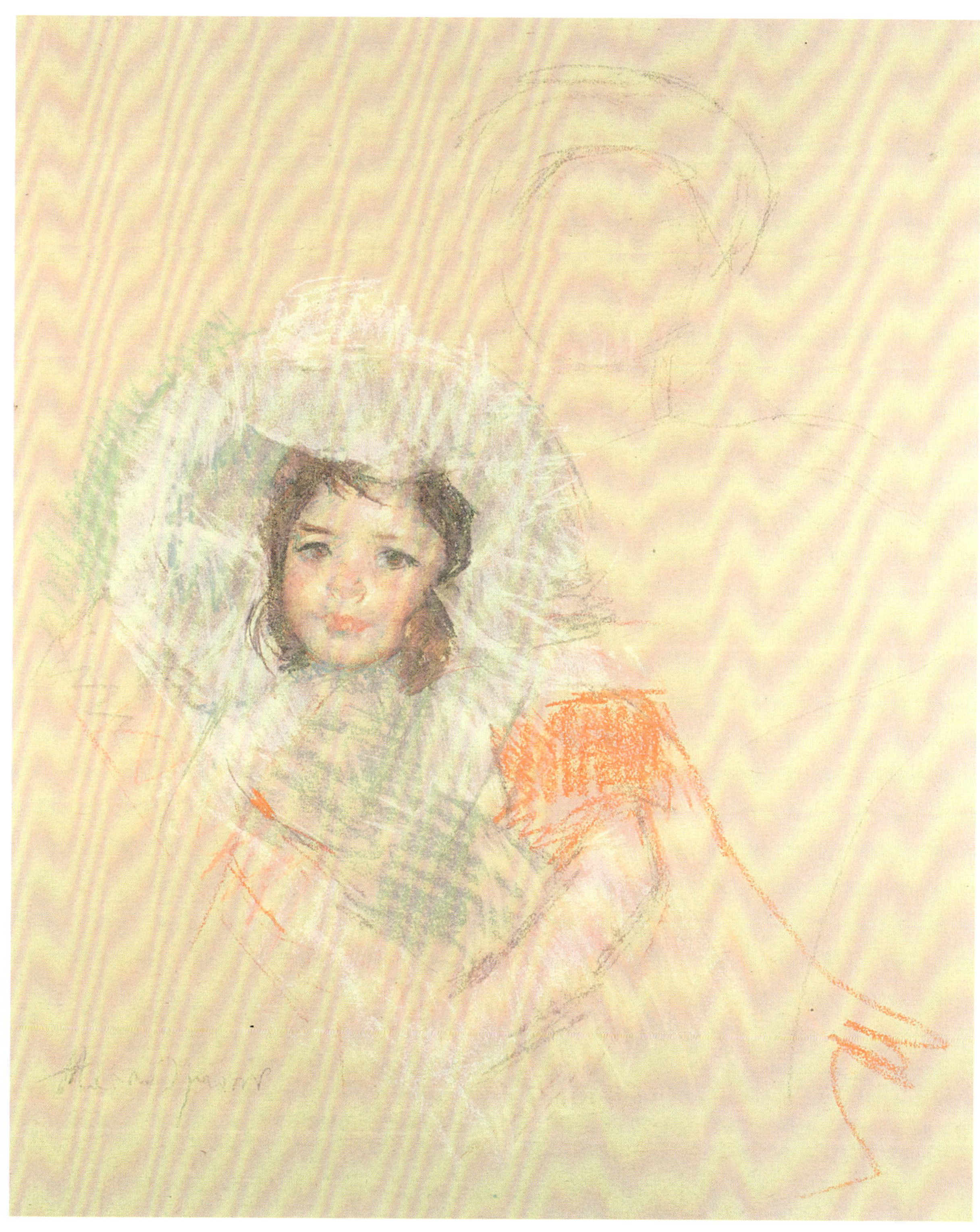

26.

Heads of Reine and of Margot

Pastel counterproof of BrCR 397
ca. 1902 [ca. 1900]
on Japan paper
with counterproof signature
25⅛ × 20½ in. (63.8 × 52 cm)

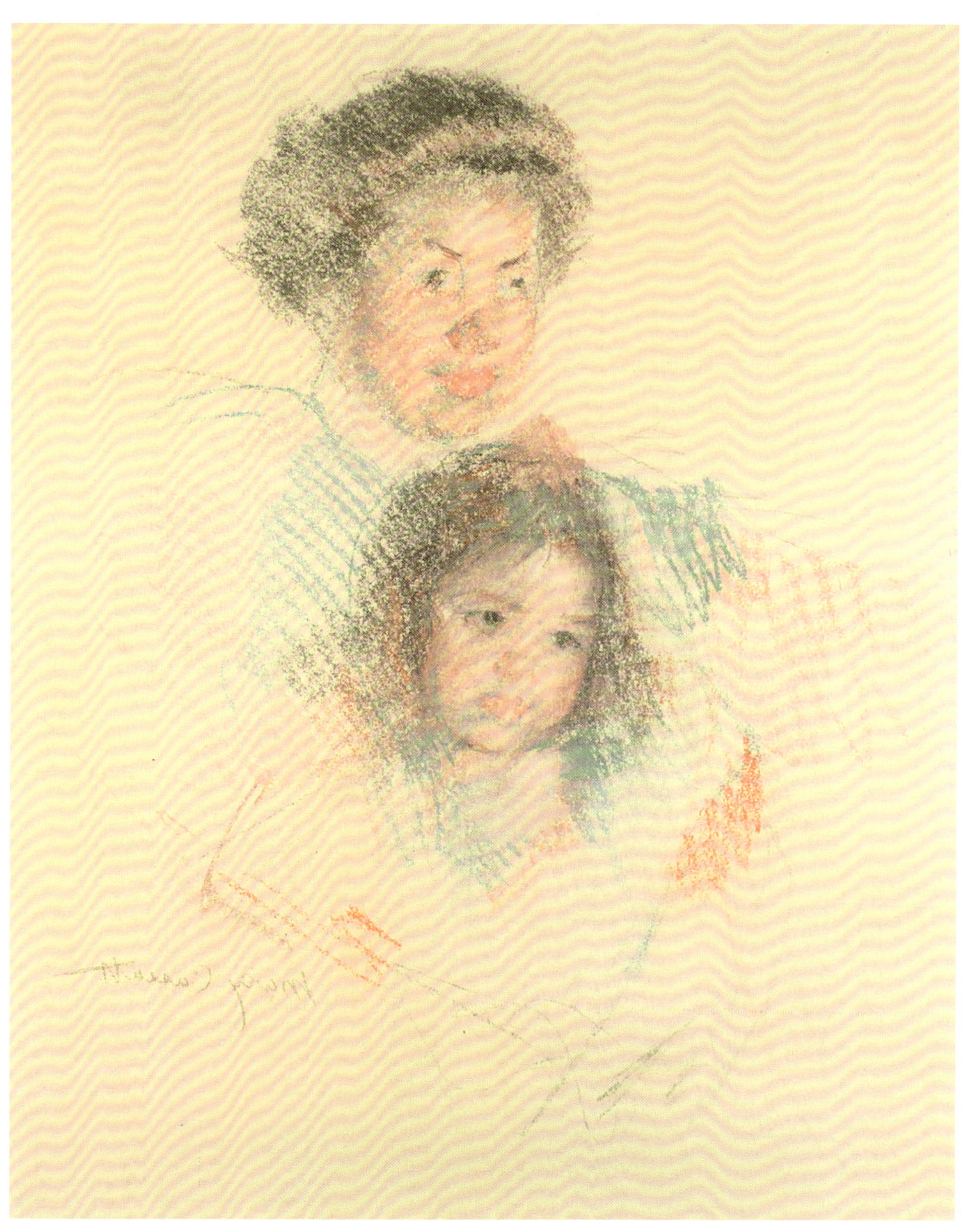

27.

Baby John on His Mother's Lap

Pastel counterproof of BrCR 576
ca. 1910 [ca. 1909–1910]
on Japan paper
with counterproof signature: M. Cassatt
32 × 24⅜ in. (81.3 × 62 cm)

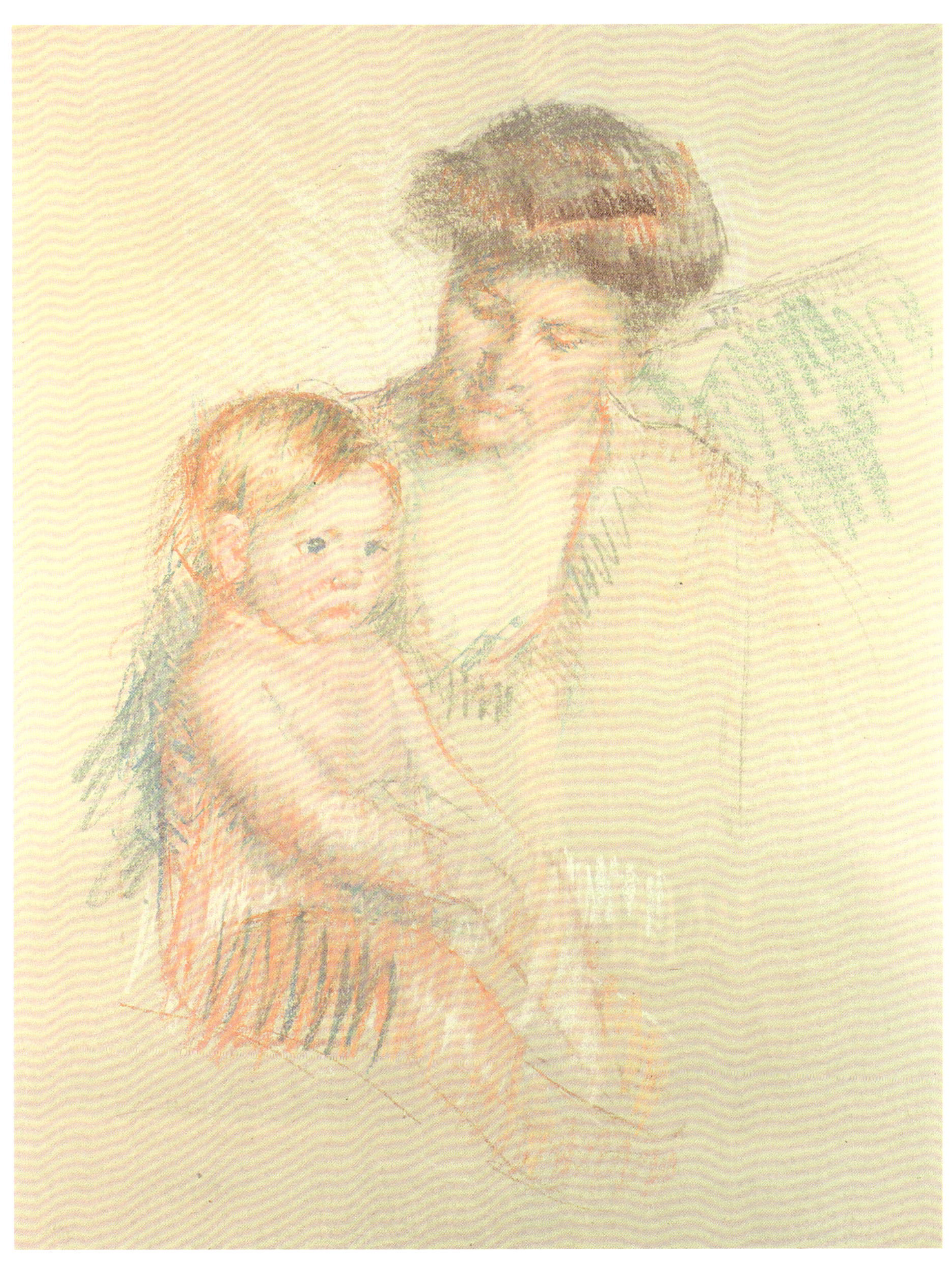

28.

Margot in a Pale Rose Hat

Pastel counterproof of an unrecorded pastel
[ca. 1902–1903]
on Japan paper
with counterproof signature
23¾ × 20¾ in. (60.3 × 52.7 cm)

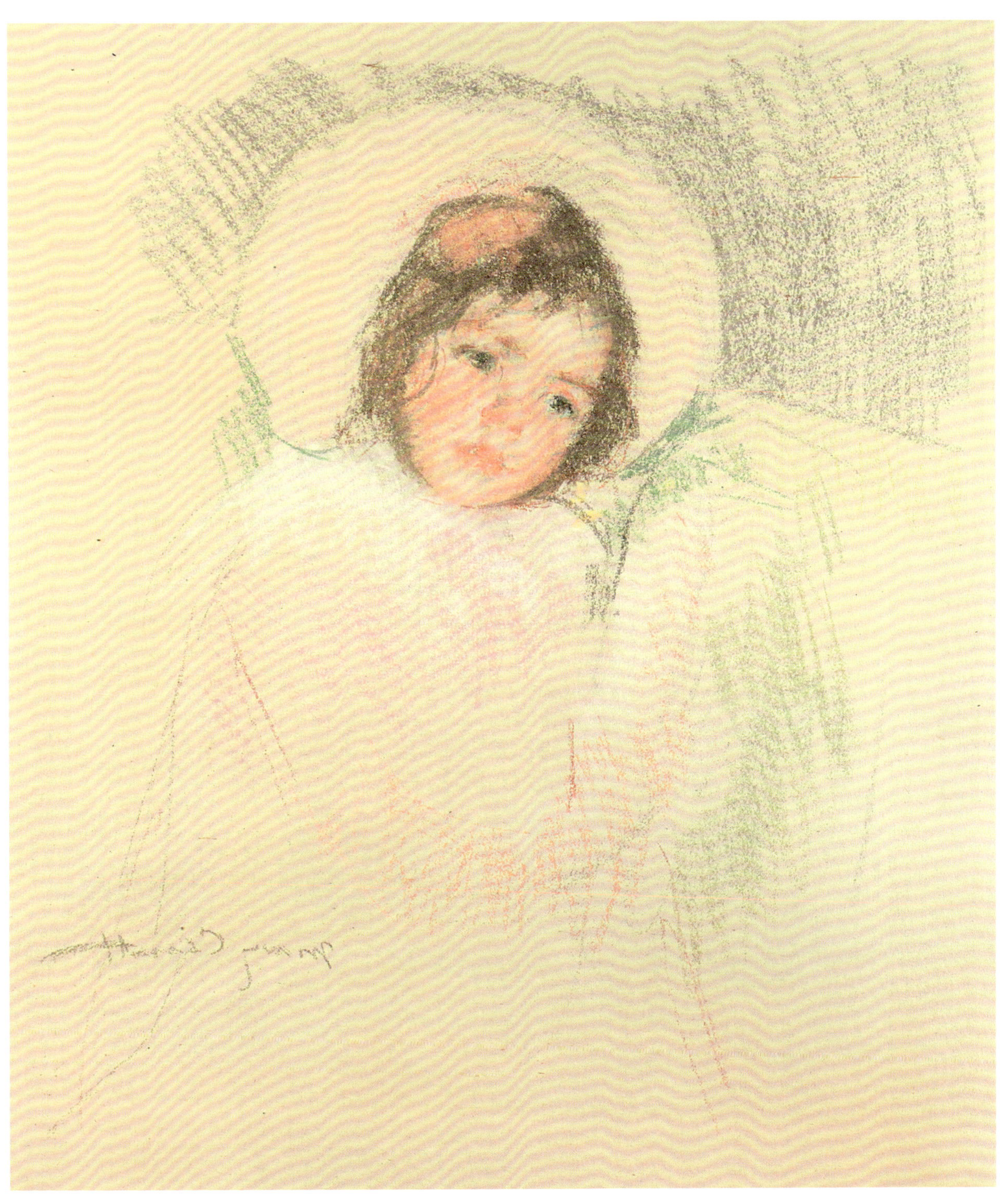

29.

Margot in a Pale Rose Hat

Pastel counterproof of an unrecorded pastel
Second impression
[ca. 1902–1903]
on Japan paper
with counterproof signature
23¾ × 20¾ in. (60.3 × 52.7 cm)

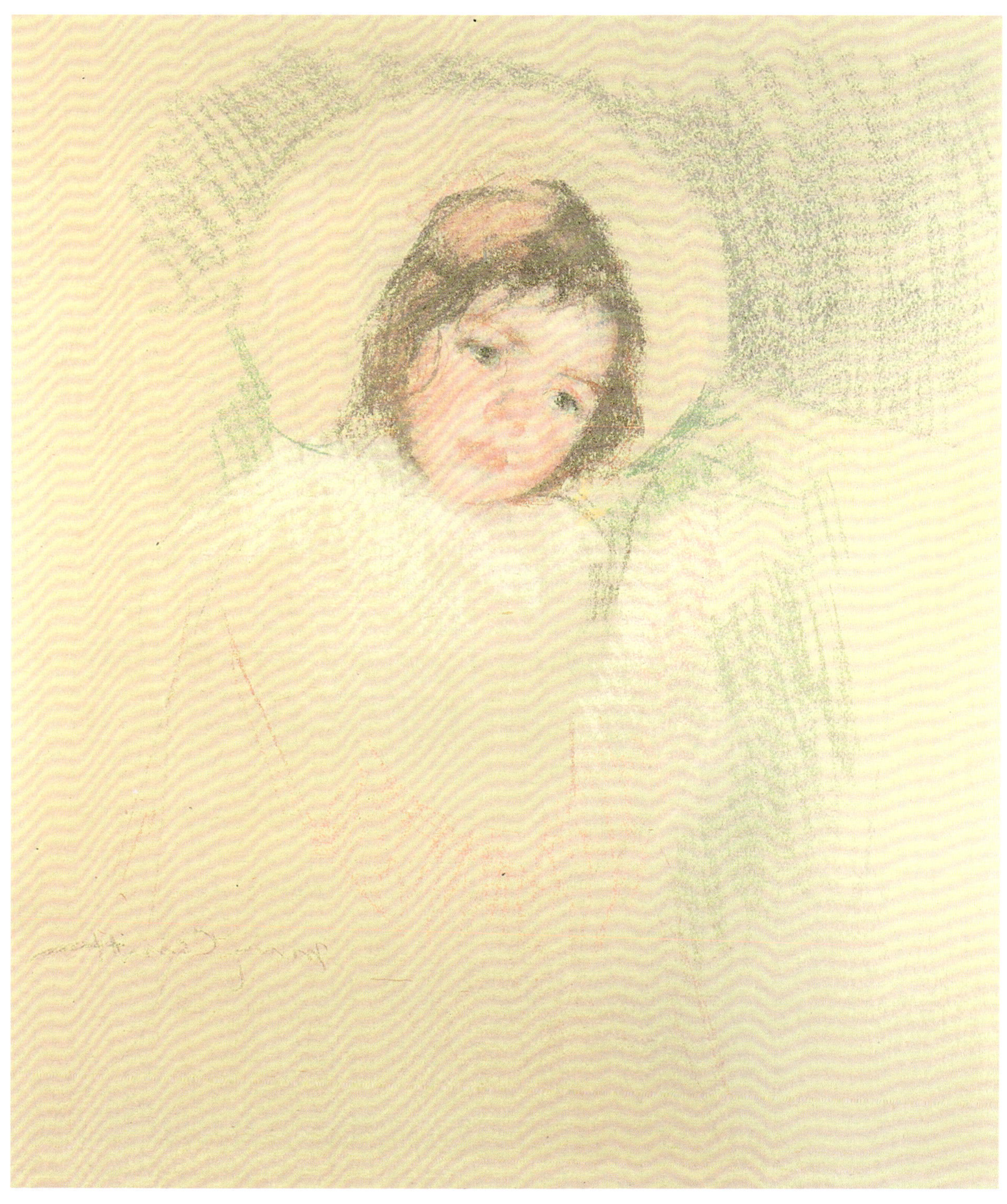

30.

Hélène of Septeuil, with a Parrot

Pastel counterproof of BrCR 184
ca. 1890 [ca. 1889–1890]
on Japan paper
with counterproof signature
27¼ × 20⅝ in. (69.2 × 52.4 cm)

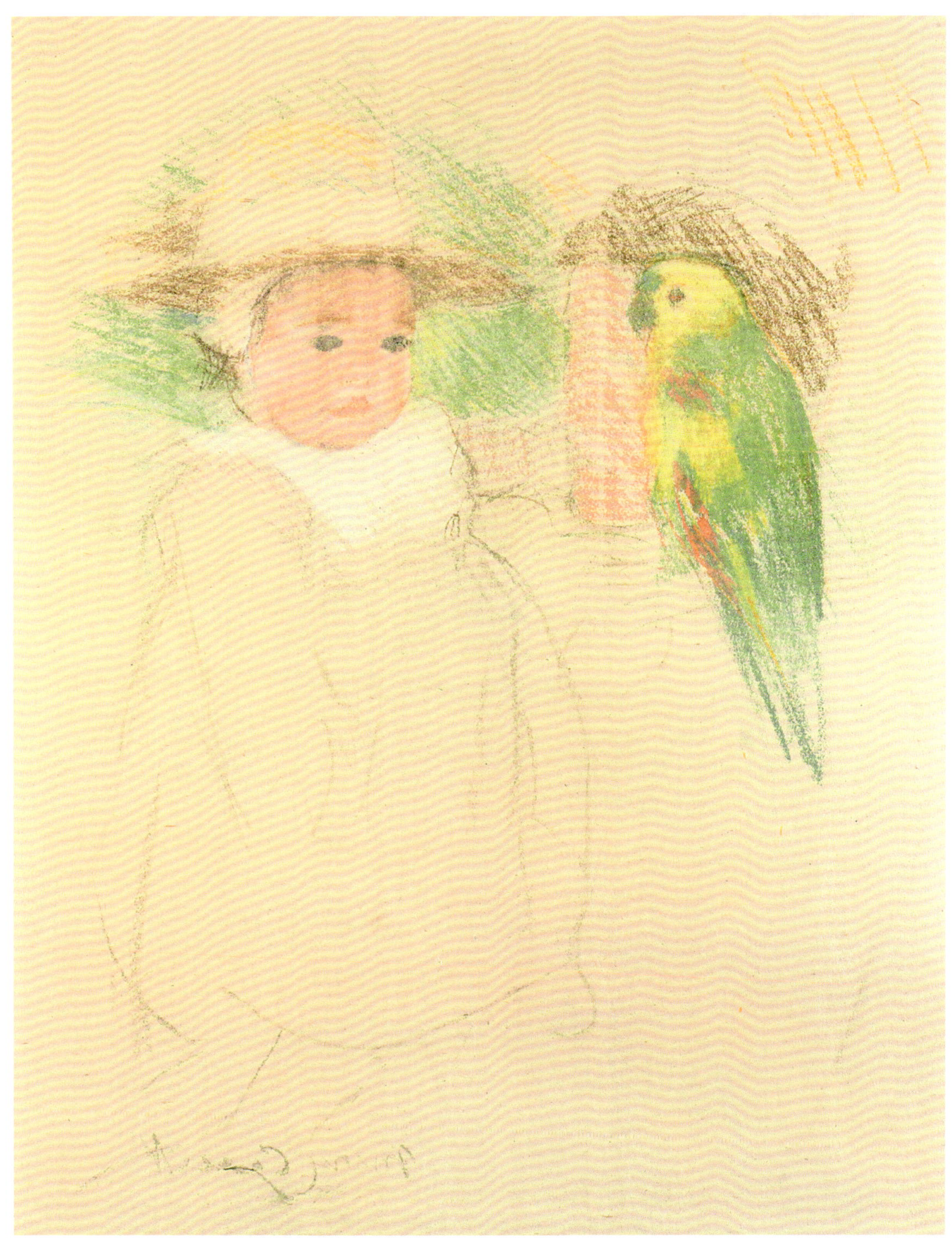

31.

Nude Dark-Eyed Little Girl with Mother in Patterned Wrapper

Pastel counterproof of an unrecorded pastel
ca. 1902 [ca. 1898–1899]
on Japan paper
with counterproof signature
26 × 22 in. (66 × 56 cm)

Another counterproof of this work, its composition
cropped, was published in Breeskin as a pastel;
see BrCR 410.

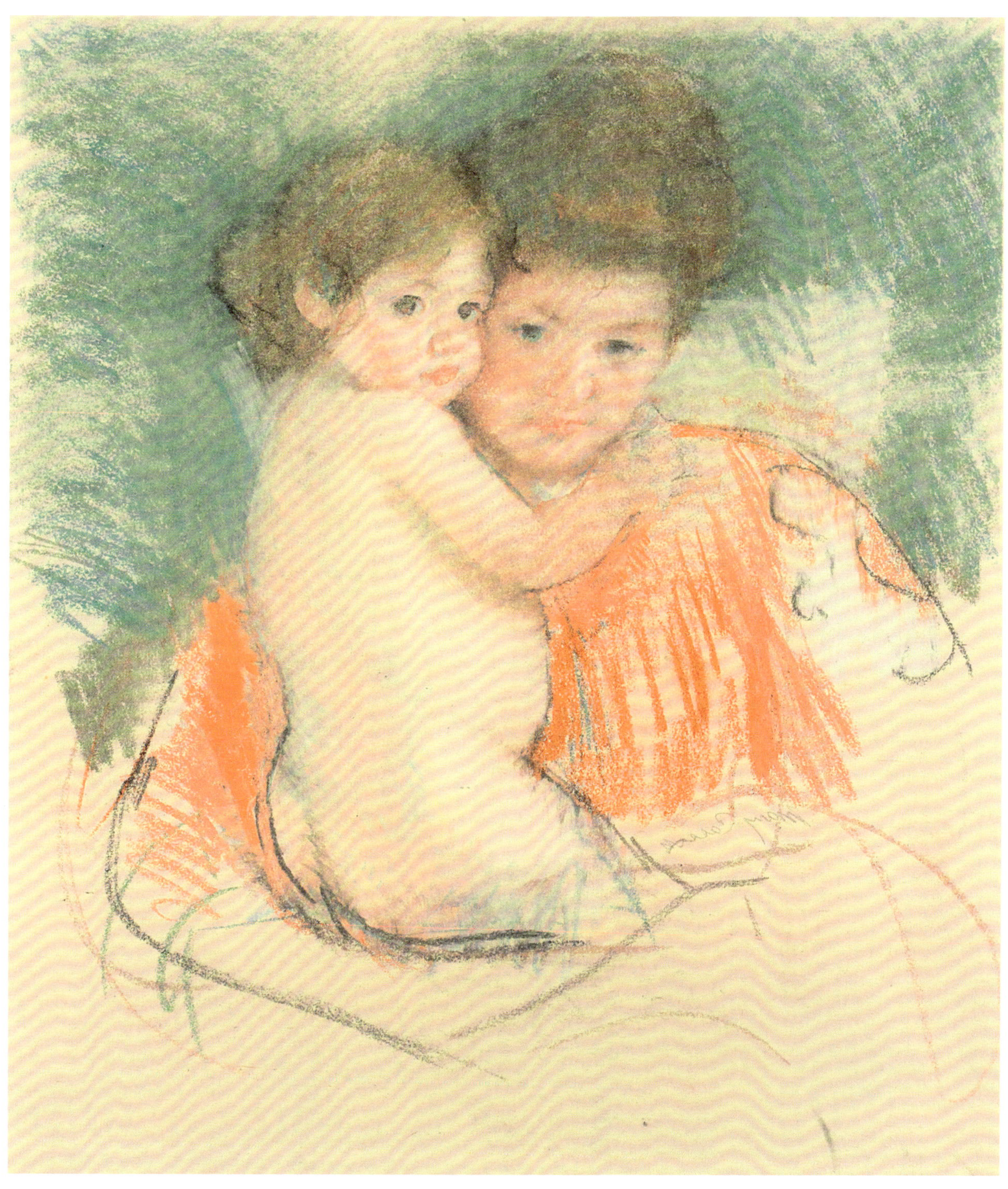

32.

Mother Louise Holding up
Her Blue-Eyed Child

Pastel counterproof of BrCR 312
ca. 1899
on Japan paper
with counterproof signature
28 × 20¾ in. (71.1 × 52.8 cm)

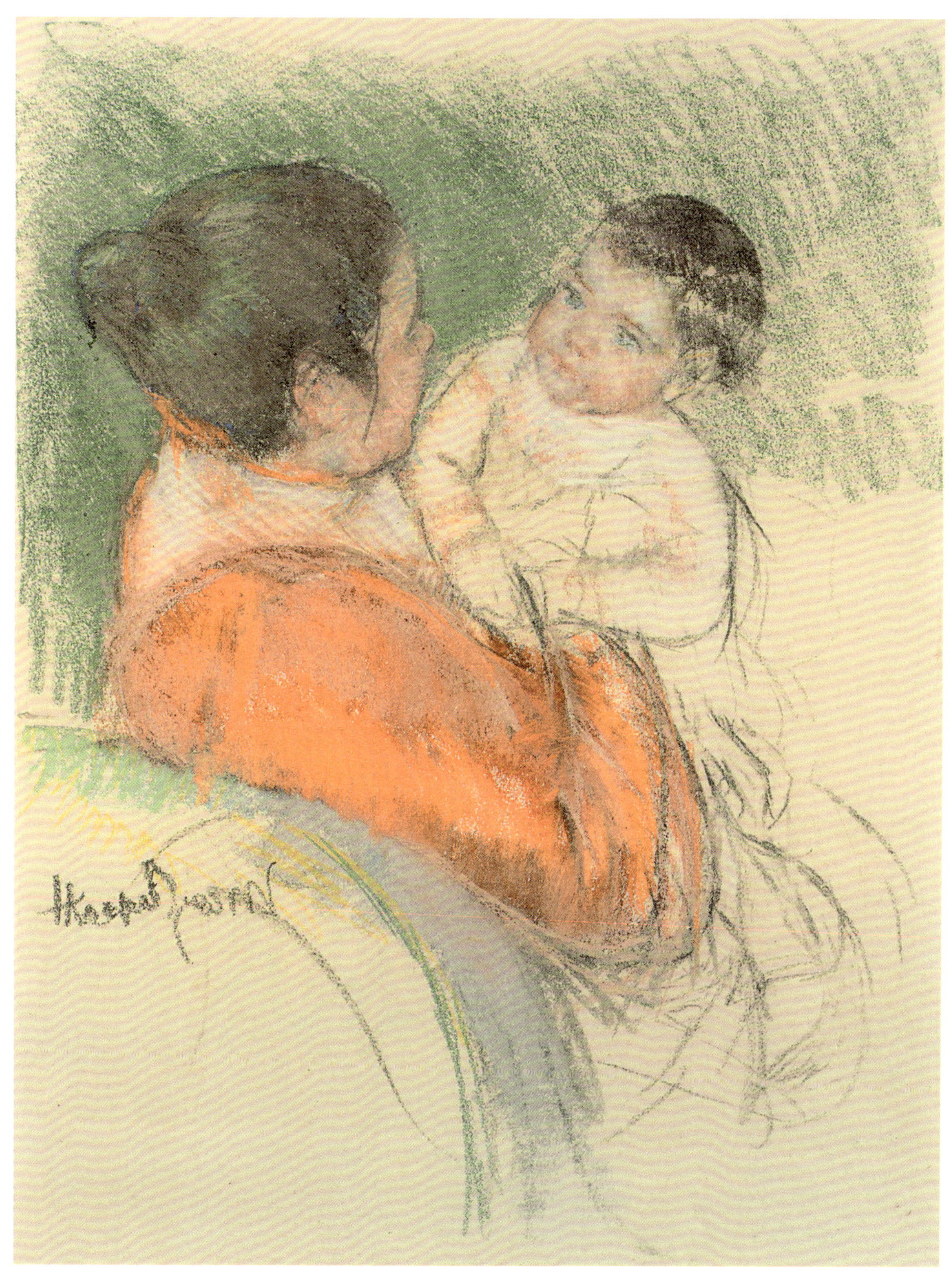

33.

Mother Rose Nursing Her Child

Pastel counterproof of BrCR 314
ca. 1900 [ca. 1908]
on Japan paper
with counterproof signature
28¾ × 24⅝ in. (73 × 62.5 cm)

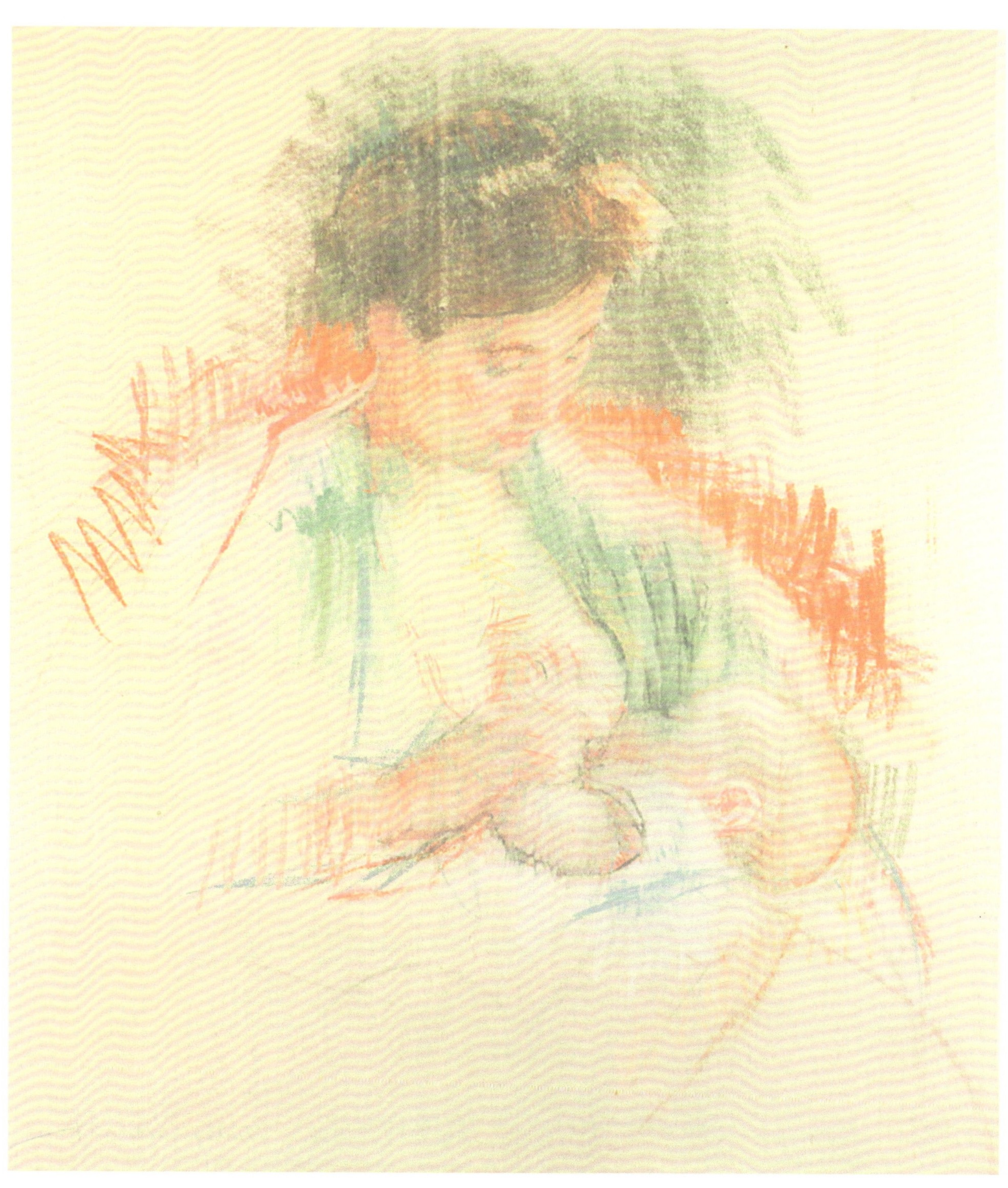

34.

Baby Embracing Her Mother

Pastel counterproof of an unrecorded pastel
[ca. 1898–1899]
on Japan paper
with counterproof signature
30½ × 25 in. (77.5 × 63.5 cm)

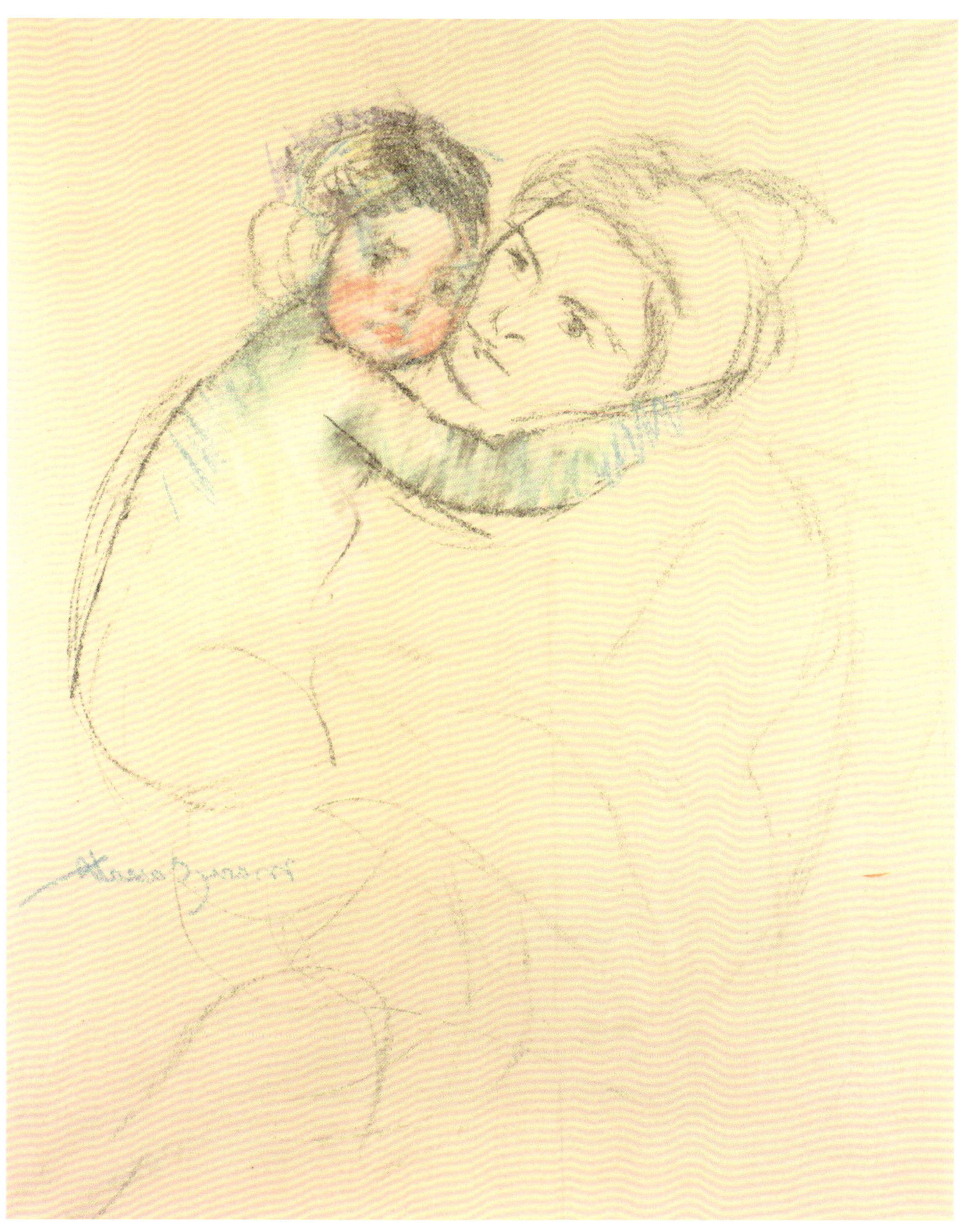

35.

Young Woman Reflecting

Pastel counterproof of BrCR 234
ca. 1894 [ca. 1894–1895]
on Japan paper
with counterproof signature
27½ × 21⅛ in. (69.8 × 53.5 cm)

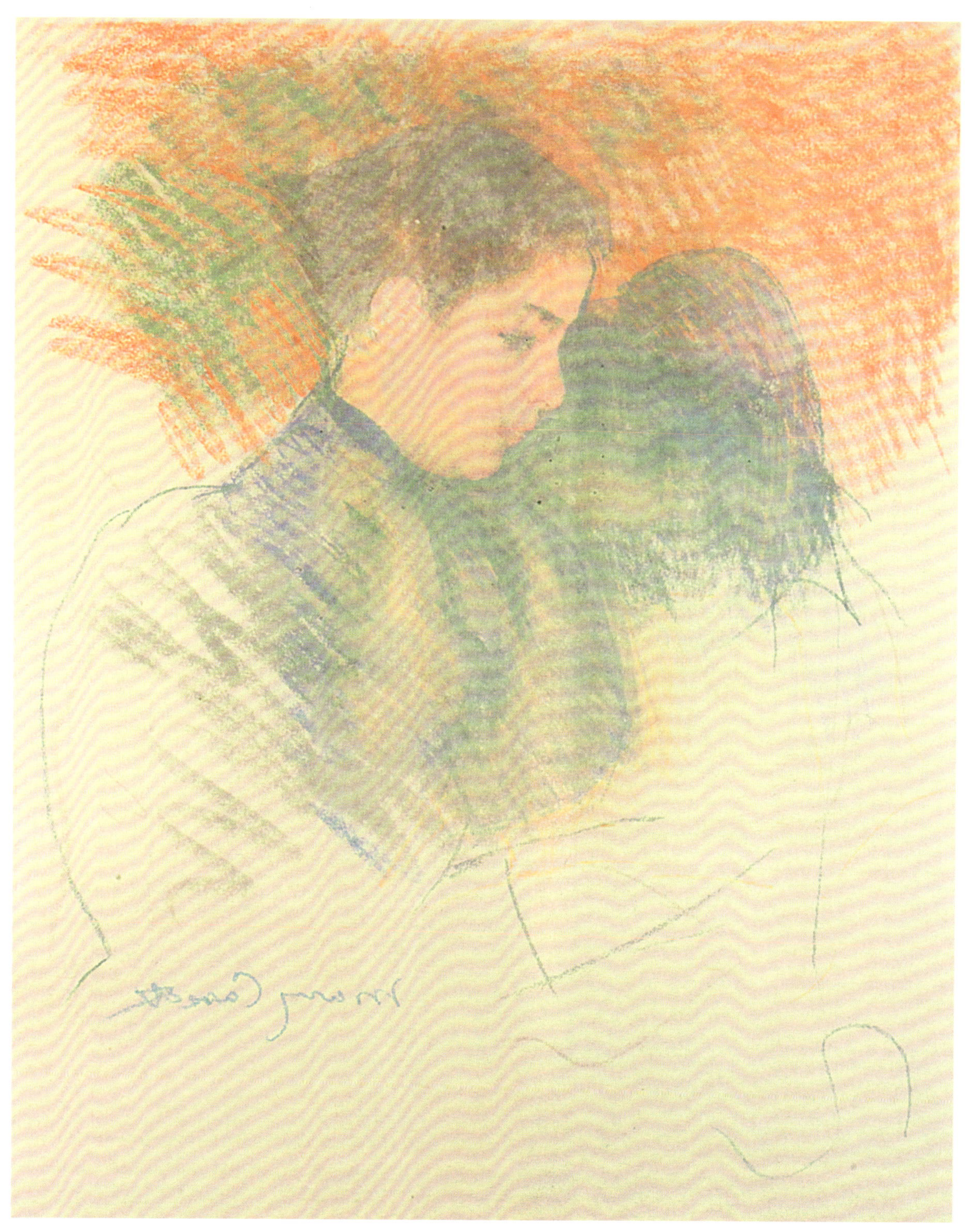

36.

Mother Jeanne Nursing Her Child (Profile Left) (No. 3)

Pastel counterproof of a work not in Breeskin
[ca. 1908]
on Japan paper
with counterproof signature
31¼ × 25 in. (79.4 × 63.5 cm)

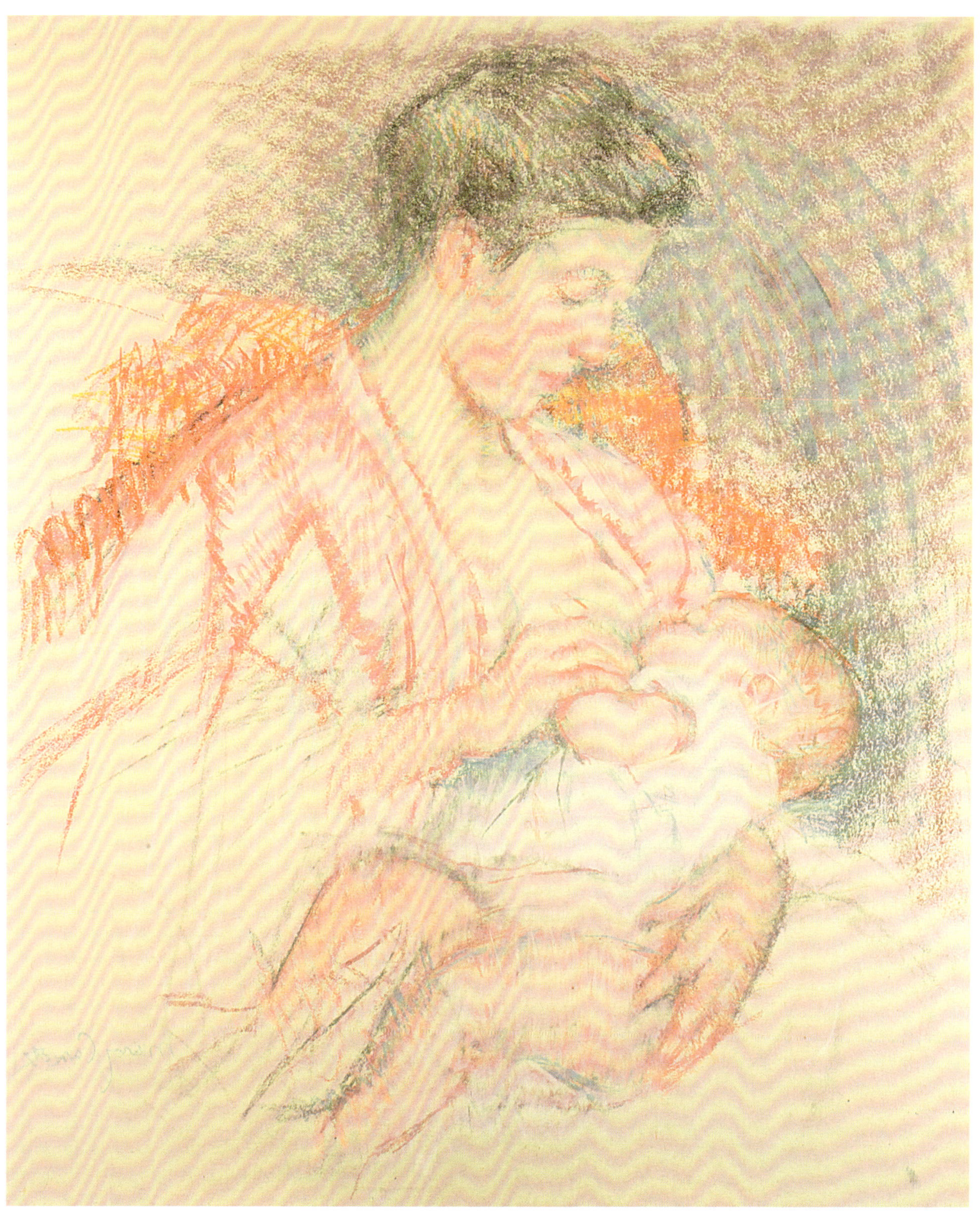

37.

Mother and Child

Pastel counterproof of a work not in Breeskin
[ca. 1908]
on Japan paper
with counterproof signature
23½ × 16¾ in. (59.7 × 42.5 cm)

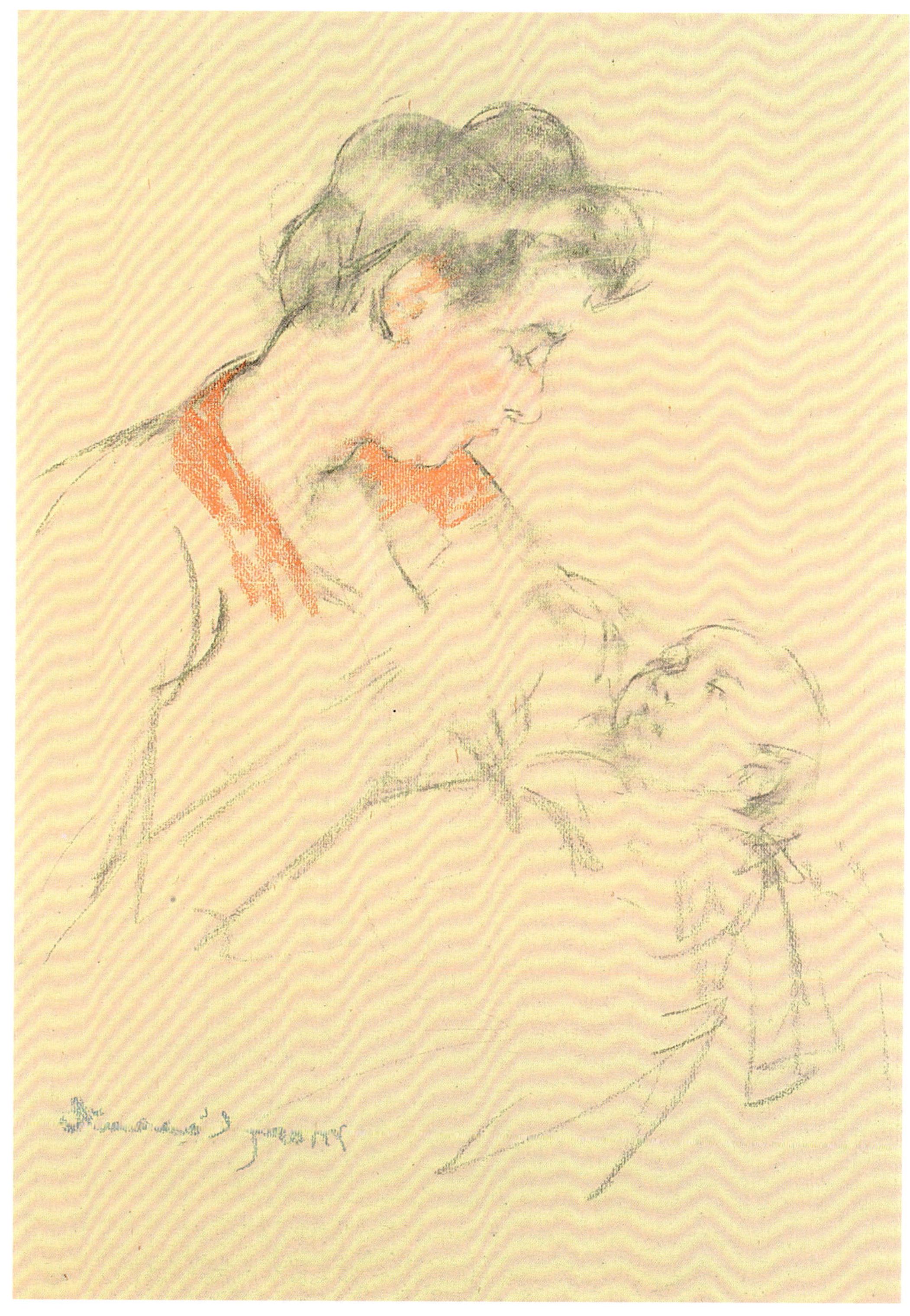

38.

Mother Jeanne Embracing Her Baby

Pastel counterproof of a work not in Breeskin
[ca. 1902–1903]
on Japan paper
with counterproof signature
31½ × 23¼ in. (80 × 59 cm)

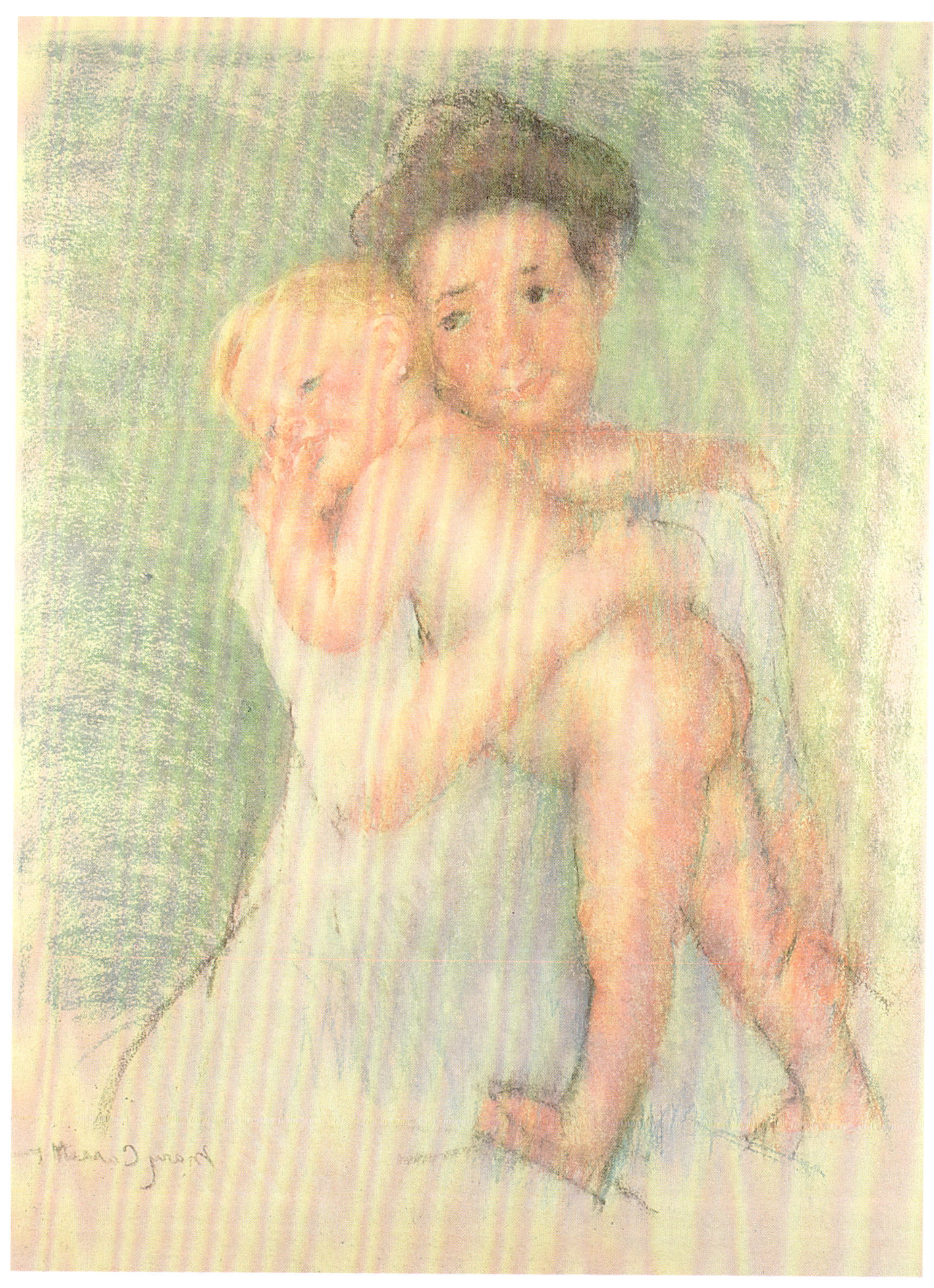

39.

Mother Holding Red-Haired Child

Pastel counterproof of an unrecorded pastel
[ca. 1901–1902]
on Japan paper
with counterproof signature
25⅛ × 20⅝ in. (63.9 × 52.5 cm)

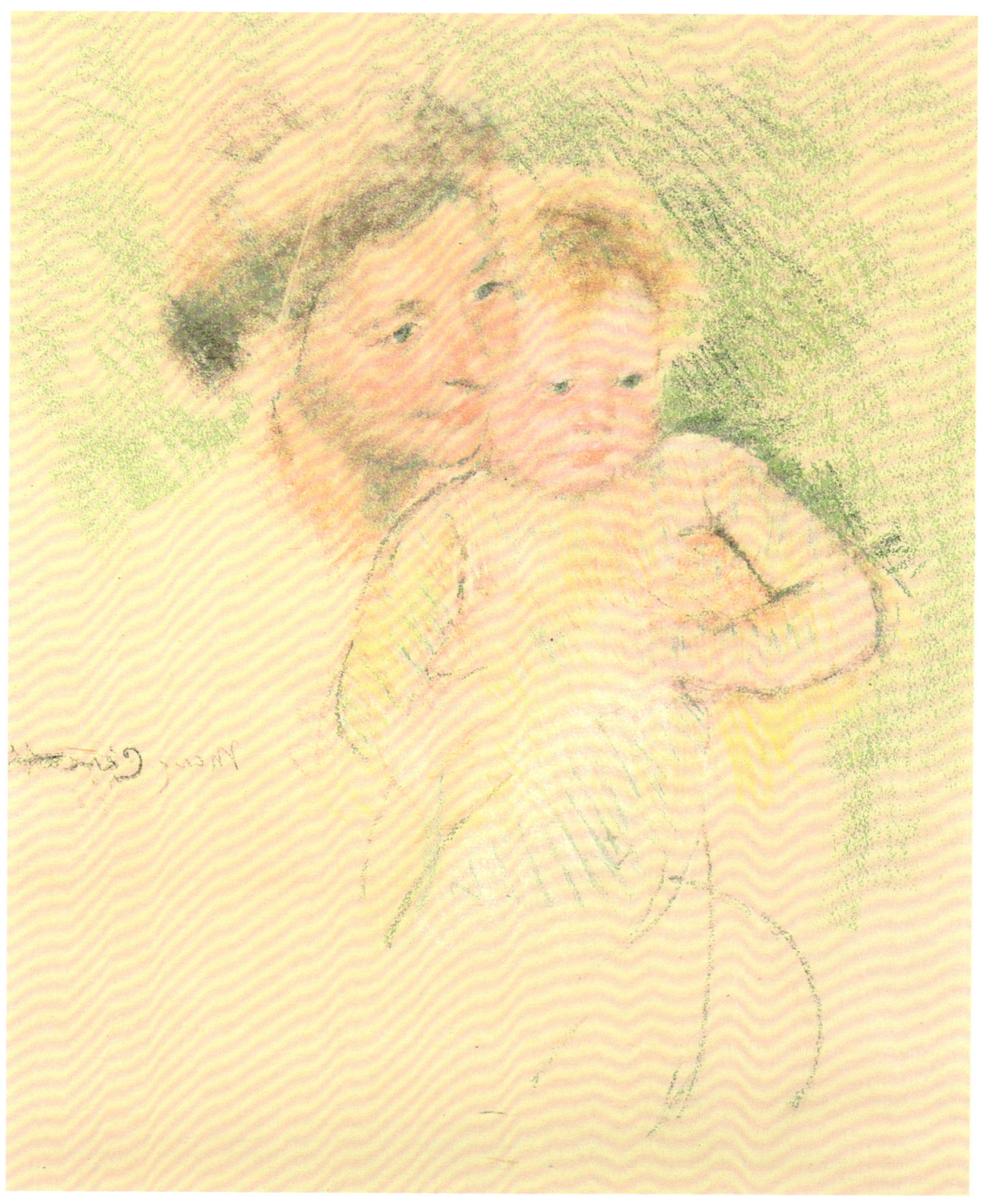

40.

Study of Sara

Pastel counterproof of a work not in Breeskin
[ca. 1900–1901]
on Japan paper
with counterproof signature
19⅝ × 17¼ in. (49.8 × 43.8 cm)

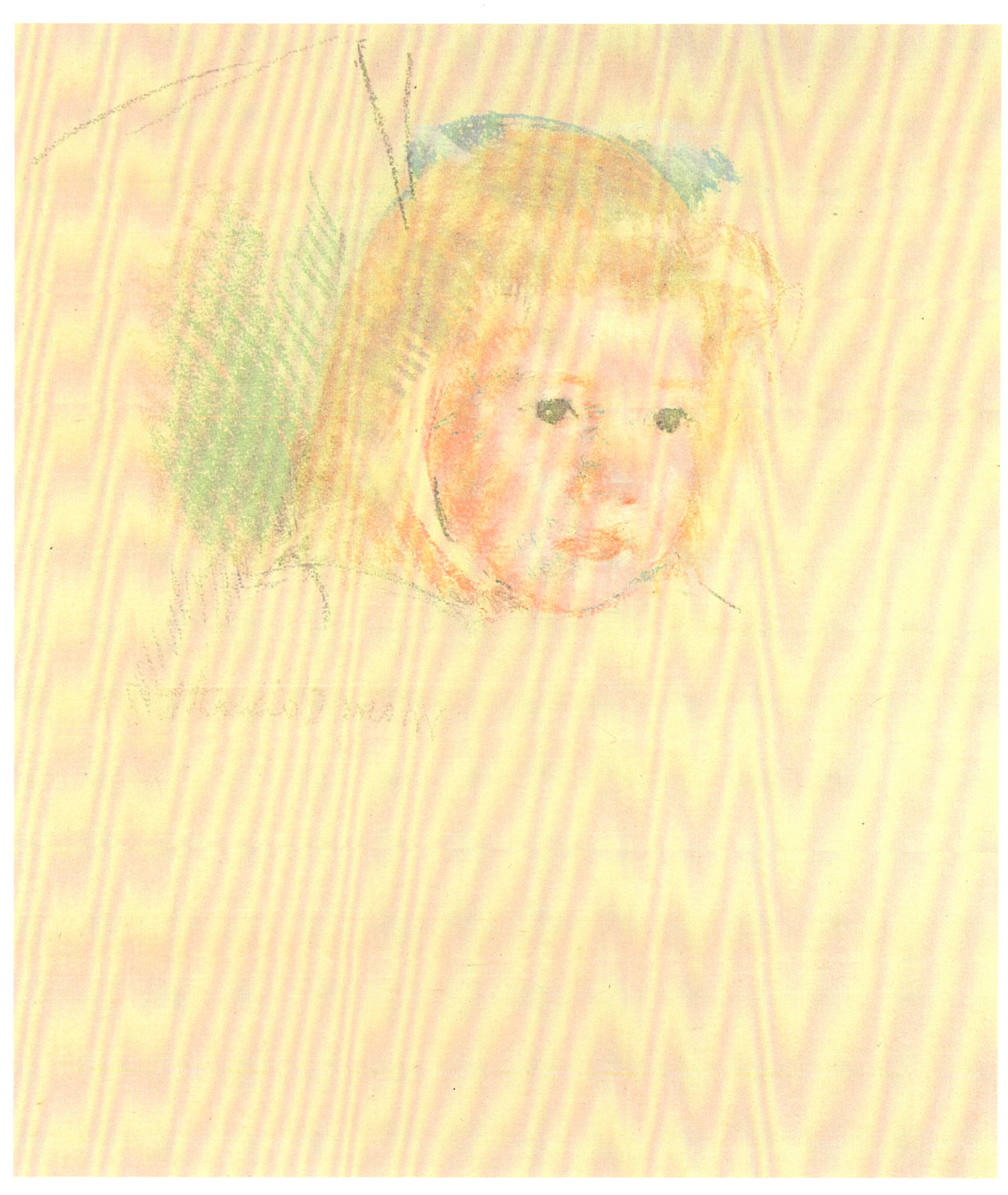

41.

Simone in a White Bonnet Seated with Clasped Hands (No. 1)

Pastel counterproof of BrCR 438
ca. 1903 [ca. 1901–1902]
on Japan paper
with counterproof signature
24¼ × 17⅝ in. (61.6 × 45 cm)

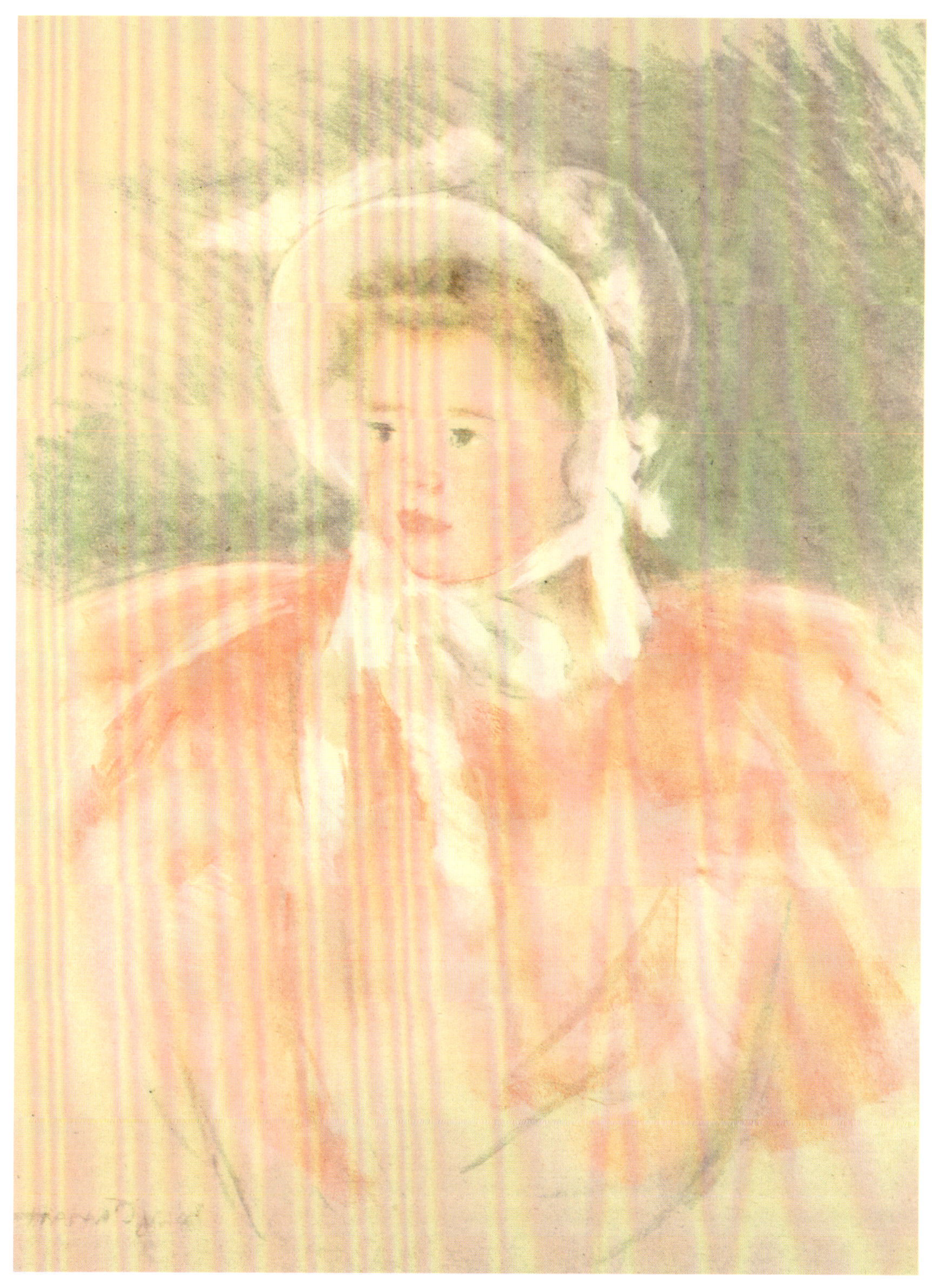

42.

Sara, in a Bonnet with Streamers Loose, and Her Dog

Pastel counterproof of BrCR 364
ca. 1901 [ca. 1901–1903]
on Japan paper
with counterproof signature
22⅜ × 16⅞ (56.8 × 42.8 cm)

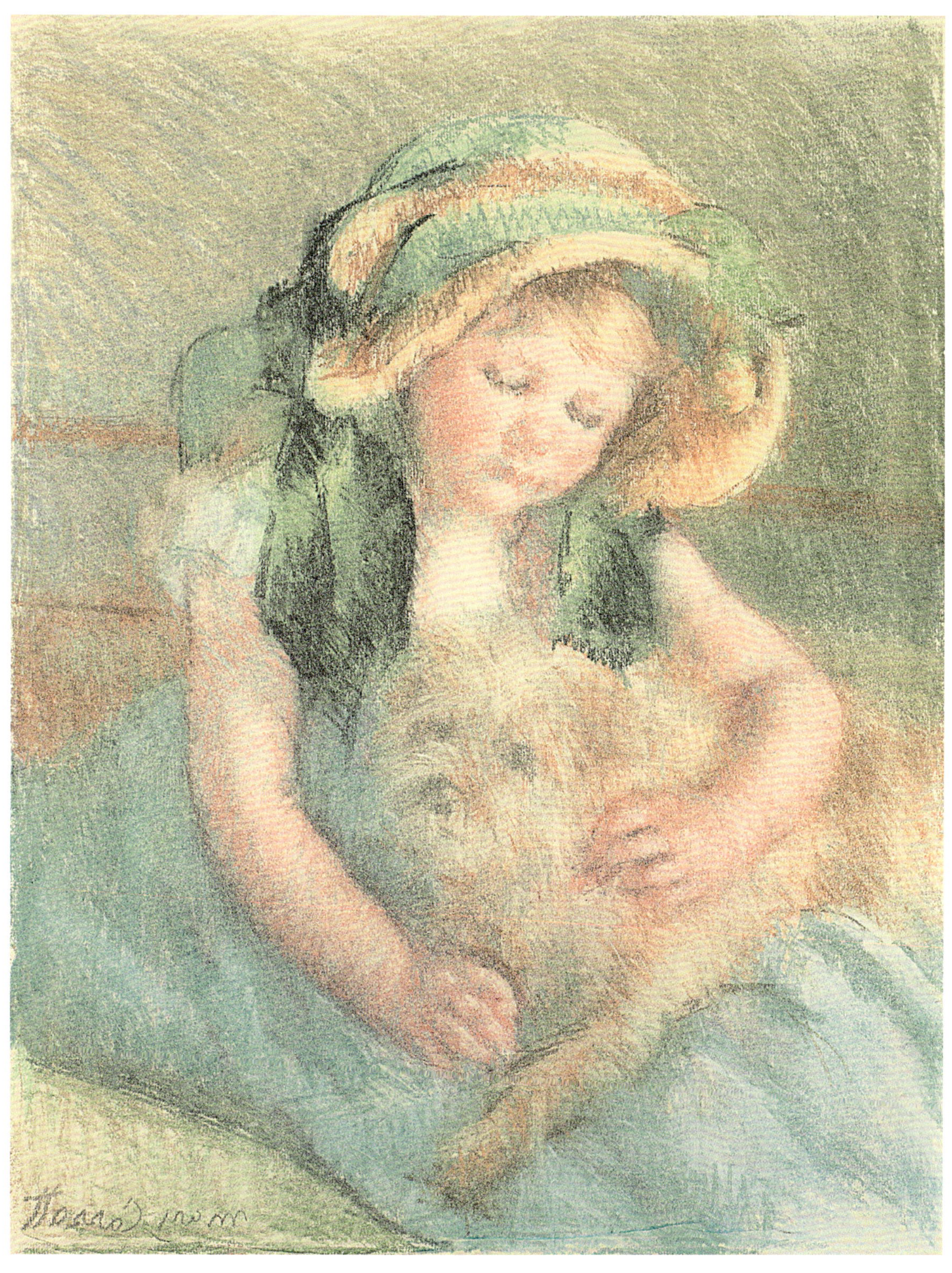

43.

Sara Looking Down at a Dog

Pastel counterproof of BrCR 356
ca. 1901 [ca. 1901–1903]
on Japan paper
with counterproof signature
22½ × 17 in. (57.2 × 43.2 cm)

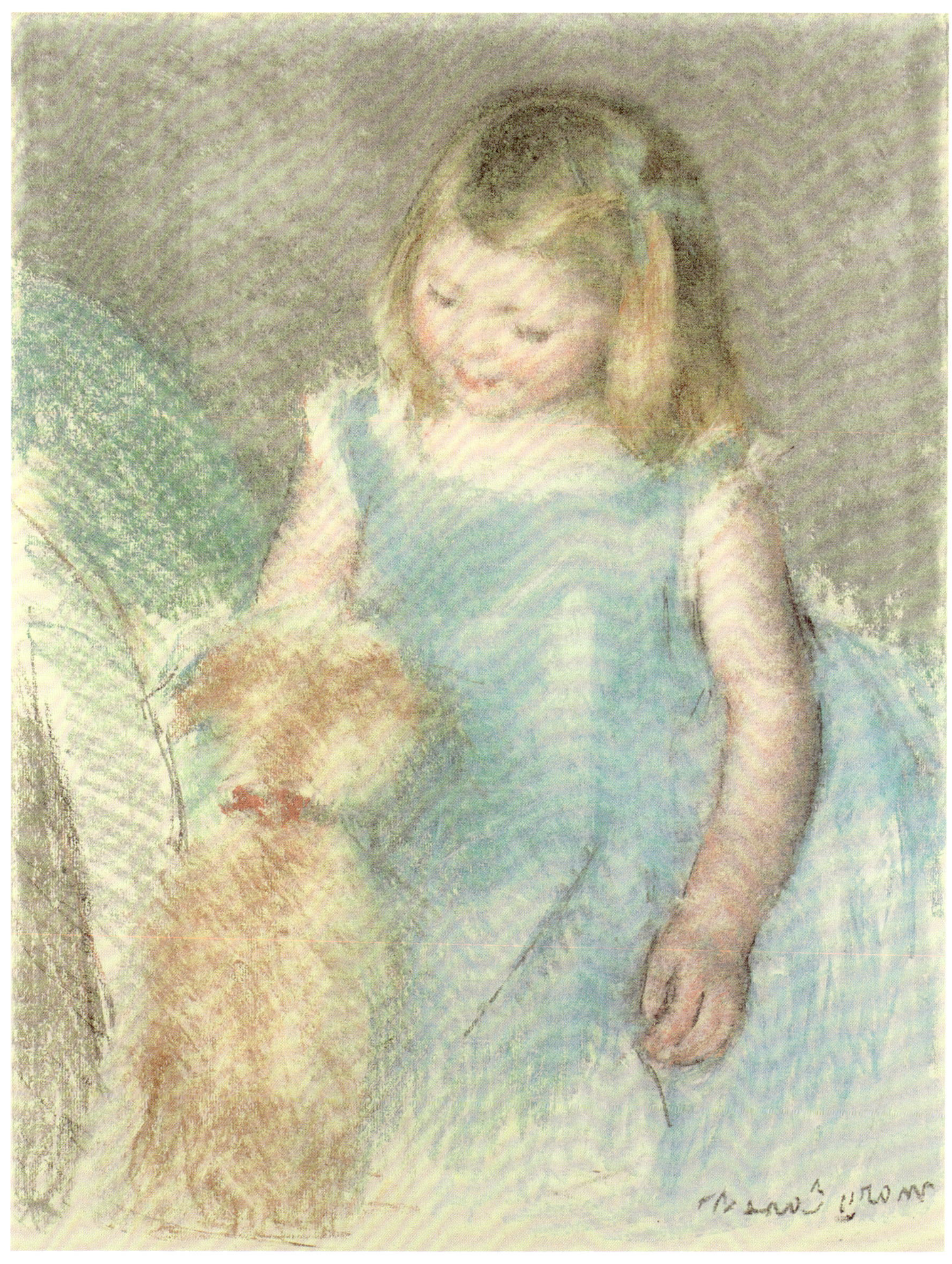

44.

Sara Wearing a Bonnet and Coat

Pastel counterproof of BrCR 454
ca. 1904 [ca. 1901–1904]
on Japan paper
with counterproof signature
24½ × 18 in. (62.2 × 45.7 cm)

The pastel from which this counterproof
was taken and a drawing, BrCr 852, are
related to the lithograph, *Sara Wearing
Her Bonnet and Coat*; see Fig. 6, p. 17.

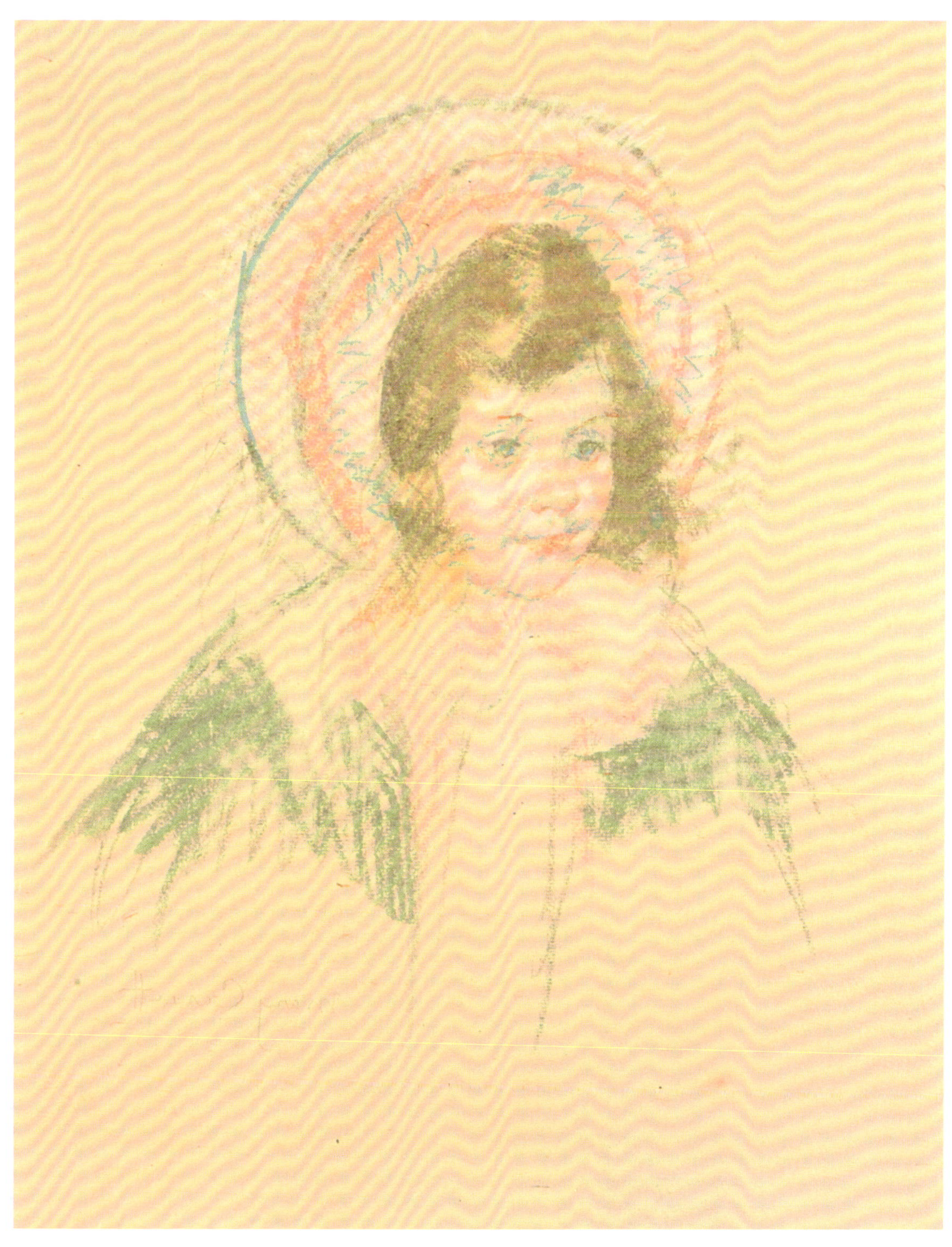

45.

Head of Margot Looking to Right

Pastel counterproof of BrCR 423
ca. 1902 [ca. 1900–1901]
on Japan paper
with counterproof signature
19⅜ × 16⅝ in. (49.2 × 42.2 cm)

The pastel, BrCR 423, now bears a
second signature.

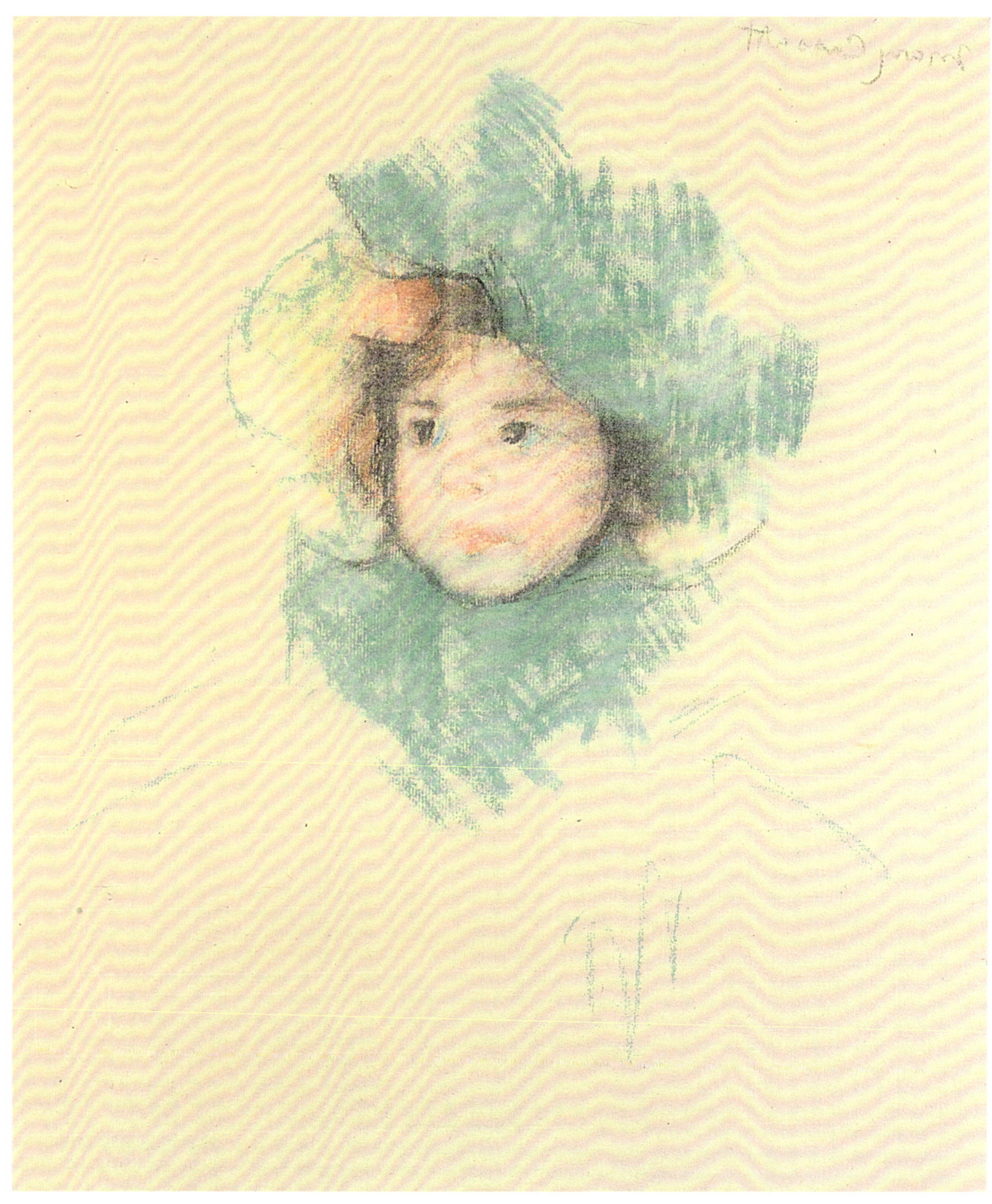

46.

Head of Adele (No. 4)

Pastel counterproof of BrCR 203
ca. 1892 [ca. 1908–1909]
on Japan paper
with counterproof signature
21¼ × 18 in. (54 × 45.7 cm)

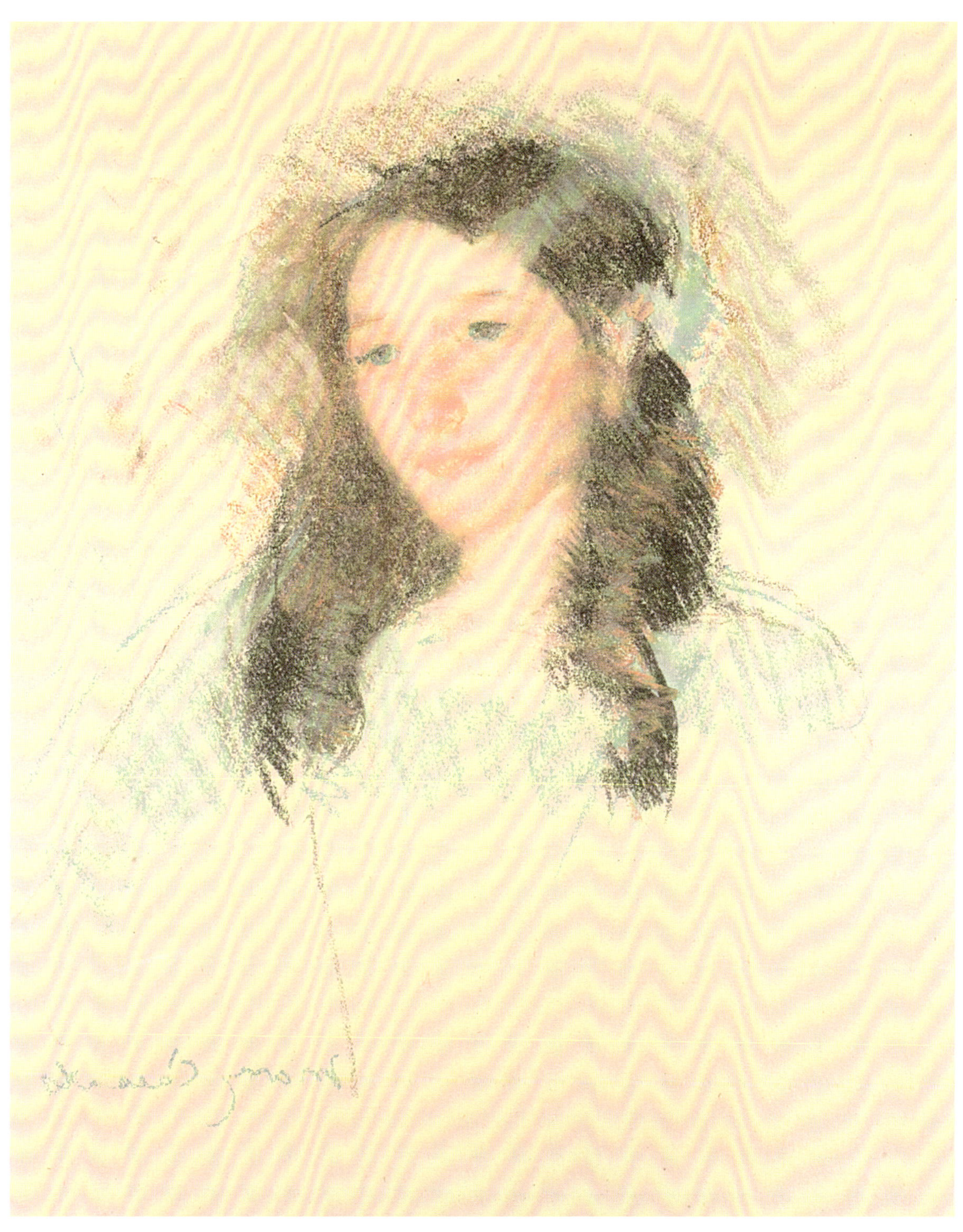

47.

Head of Adele (No. 3)

Pastel counterproof of BrCR 202
1892 [ca. 1908–1909]
on Japan paper
with counterproof signature
21½ × 18 in. (54.6 × 45.7 cm)

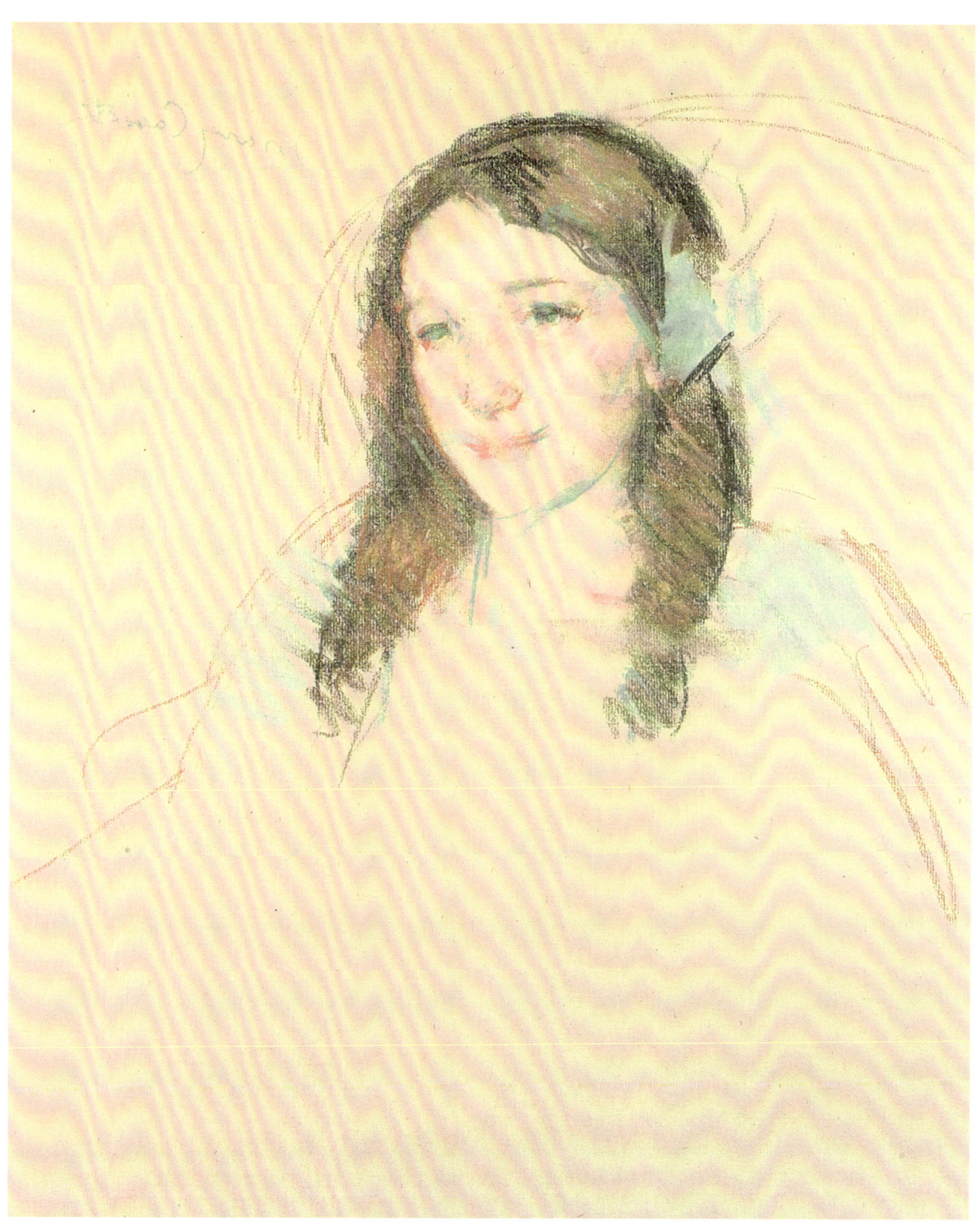

48.

Sketch of Woman in Light Green Wrapper Holding Her Child

Pastel counterproof of BrCR 411
ca. 1902 [ca. 1898–1899]
on Japan paper
with counterproof signature
24¾ × 20¾ in. (63 × 53 cm)

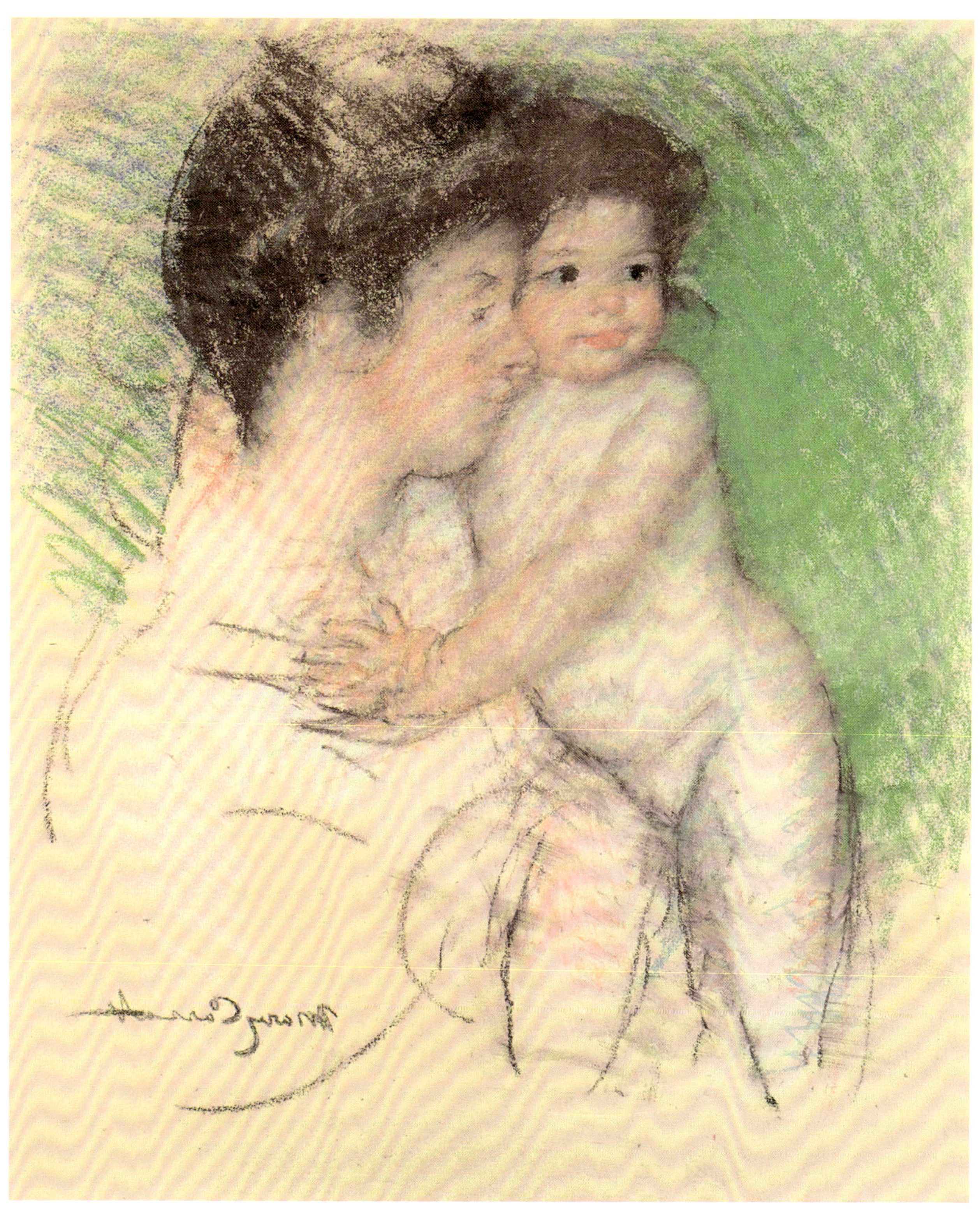

Index to Illustrations

Numbers refer to catalogue numbers

Contributors

Warren Adelson is President of Adelson Galleries and a member of the catalogue raisonné committees for John Singer Sargent and Mary Cassatt. He has contributed to, among other publications, *Childe Hassam, Impressionist; Sargent Abroad: Figures and Landscapes; John Singer Sargent's "El Jaleo"; Sargent's Women*; and *Mary Cassatt, Prints and Drawings from the Artist's Studio.*

Marc Rosen and **Susan Pinsky** are private art dealers and experts in prints and drawings. Mr. Rosen was Senior Vice President at Sotheby's, where he reorganized the Print Department globally and became senior expert in the Department of Impressionist and Modern Paintings, Drawings and Sculpture. Ms. Pinsky, who was trained as an artist, is a former Director of Sotheby's Print Department in New York. Rosen and Pinsky have presented numerous exhibitions at Adelson Galleries, including *Mary Cassatt, Prints and Drawings from the Artist's Studio* and *French Prints of the Late 19th Century*, and exhibitions of the works of Gauguin, Pissarro, Redon, Matisse, and Picasso.

Jay E. Cantor, Director of the Mary Cassatt Catalogue Raisonné Committee, has written *Winterthur* and contributed to *Childe Hassam, Impressionist* and *Mary Cassatt, Prints and Drawings from the Artist's Studio*. He established the American Paintings Department at Christie's and was founding president of the Georgia O'Keeffe Museum in Santa Fe, New Mexico.

Pamela A. Ivinski, Ph.D., is a member of the Mary Cassatt Catalogue Raisonné Committee and serves as the Committee's Senior Research Associate. Co-author of *Maurice Prendergast: Paintings of America*, she completed a dissertation on Cassatt's maternal imagery in 2003 and has published many articles on graphic design and popular culture.

This book was designed and produced by Marcus Ratliff Inc. in New York.
Color imaging by Center Page in West Seneca, New York.

5,000 copies have been printed by Meridian Printing, East Greenwich, Rhode Island.

October 2004

The counterproofs were photographed by Gilles de Fayet in Paris (gillesdefayet.com).

Digital photography, pages 17 and 25: Martin Senn
Digital photography, pages 13–15, 24, 26, and 28: Timothy Pyle, Light Blue Studio
Photograph, page 16: courtesy of Mary Cassatt Catalogue Raisonné Committee